D1336651

DANOLI

Also by Michael Taub

JACK DOYLE – FIGHTING FOR LOVE

DANOLI
The People's Champion

Tom Foley and Michael Taub

First published in Great Britain in 1997 by Robson Books Ltd,
Bolsover House, 5-6 Clipstone Street, London W1P 8LE

British Library Cataloguing in Publication Data
A catalogue record for this title is available from the British Library

ISBN 1 86105 109 3

Typeset by FSH Ltd., London.
Printed in Great Britain by Butler & Tanner Ltd.,
London and Frome

For

SHANE BRODERICK

whose courage in adversity is

an inspiration to us all

Contents

A Very Special Breed ix
Acknowledgements xi
Prologue: They Shoot Horses, Don't They? 1
1 Danoli the Brave 3
2 Getting Going and Tipping Around 10
3 The Bone-setter Gets His Horse 24
4 We Say 'No' to Charlie (Haughey, That Is) 33
5 Cheltenham Goes Hoarse Over Danoli 44
6 With a Little Help from My Friend 56
7 The Call That Broke My Heart 62
8 The Challenge I Could Not Ignore 65
9 He's Coming Home! 76
10 Tears and Cheers as Danoli Battles Back 81
11 I'll Never Ask Charlie Again 95
12 Gold Strike in the Hennessy 105
13 Danny Boy has the Gift 117
14 Hanging On for The Grip 133
15 We Click with the Camera Lads 138
16 Who the Hell is Boris? 145
17 Bless this Horse 151

18	Top of the Form	153
19	Operation Newmarket	157
20	Danoli's Kingdom	166
The Last Word		175
Glossary		177
Danoli on the Record		179
Meet the Family		182
Index		183

A Very Special Breed

To get a horse out in front and bring him home first past the post is not just the work of one man and never can be. Especially a horse who has become one of the biggest celebrities in the history of racing. More, it is the belief and commitment of an entire family of racing folk, friends and neighbours who have inspired Danoli or been inspired by him. Many of them are nameless but I would like to thank the following people who have helped make the past five years the most memorable of my life:

My wife, Goretti, and children Sharon, Adrienne, Goretti and Patrick;

Danoli's larger-than-life owner, Danny O'Neill, whose willingness to put his money where my mouth was started us off on a journey neither of us would have dreamed possible;

Our dedicated team of work riders, especially Noel (Hammie) Hamilton, who rides out Danoli each day, was crushed when the horse fell on him and yet was glad it was he who was injured and not Danoli;

Two great trainers – Jim Bolger, a big man with a generous heart who asks nothing in return, and Paddy Mullins, a genius and a gentleman;

Our loyal group of owners, who have stuck by us through all the hard times;

Chris Riggs and the staff at Leahurst veterinary hospital;

The children and teachers of St Finian's for their prayers and their cards;

Fr Edward Dowling, for his many blessings;

Little Paul Minchin, for his devotions from Lourdes;

Padge Gill, a loyal and trusty helper in the early days;

The Turf Club, for their patience and understanding;

Finally, Danoli himself and those people everywhere who have sent letters and cards and telephoned to pledge their love and support for this wonderful horse.

TOM FOLEY

Acknowledgements

Thanks are also due to the following for their help and co-operation:

Kate Mills of Robson Books, Steve Delve of *The Sporting Life*, Padraig English, Joe Fallon, David O'Connor, John Foley, Ger Foley, Pat Foley, Barney Cordell-Lavarack, Jim Gaul, Ger Donoghoe, Michael O'Neill, John Walsh, Rory Whelan, Martha Taub.

Prologue

They Shoot Horses, Don't They?

IT WAS like a scene straight out of *Die Hard*. The only thing missing was the sound of gunfire raking the tall, forbidding buildings huddled together as if for comfort along the winding avenues. Blue light flashing, siren wailing and flanked by police outriders, the ambulance cut a swathe through the busy early evening traffic, ignoring lights set at red and scattering startled pedestrians as it hurtled on towards the outskirts of the city.

But these weren't the mean streets of Brooklyn or the Bronx and the cops weren't wearing the gleaming silver badges of the NYPD. This was Liverpool, and there was drama and desperation in the air as the ambulance transported its precious cargo in a life-or-death race against time. Down into the bowels beneath the River Mersey it sped, the high pitch of the siren ear-splitting in its intensity as it reverberated from the closed-in walls and ceiling of the tunnel, its blue light and those of the police motor cycles transformed into dozens of dazzling neon signs.

Finally the convoy emerged into the fading sunlight of the Wirral Peninsula and zoomed on down the M53 motorway, heading due south. At Junction 3 it veered off and made for Leahurst, its destination near Neston in the South Wirral where the Philip Leverhulme Large Animal Hospital – a University of Liverpool veterinary field station – was waiting to receive its VIP patient.

Danoli, the People's Champion, revered on both sides of the Irish Sea and glorious winner this Grand National day in 1995 of the Martell Aintree Hurdle, had shattered a bone in his leg. They shoot horses, don't they? Horses with career-threatening injuries that can so easily turn them into unwanted cripples? Mostly they do. But Danoli was lucky. Lucky to have an owner like Danny O'Neill. Lucky to be in the best place it was possible for an injured animal to be.

The hospital's resident in equine orthopaedics, Yvonne Rice, and the duty senior clinician, Dr Derek Knottenbelt, were on red alert and primed for action. They began an urgent examination of the horse. There was nothing to do but wait and worry and wonder.

Wonder how a day that had started so rich in promise could have gone so horribly, tragically wrong.

1
Danoli the Brave

DANOLI had been out to restore his reputation after finishing third in the Smurfit Champion Hurdle at Cheltenham three weeks earlier. His preparation for the Champion had been interrupted through illness and he'd failed to run his true race. Redemption was at hand at Aintree in an event he'd also won in 1994, shortly after his stupendous success in the Sun Alliance Hurdle at Cheltenham. But the presence in the Martell of arch rival Dorans Pride – tough, classy and consistent – cast a shadow over his chances.

There'd been an element of bad blood between the two camps. And Dorans Pride, trained in Ireland by Michael Hourigan, had added spice to the contest by winning the Bonusprint Stayers' Hurdle at Cheltenham. The gauntlet was down.

Yet talk of a two-horse race would have been glibly self-indulgent – an insult to the connections of the remainder of the runners in an event containing a cast-list of star names. Danoli and Dorans Pride would hardly have things their own way with the likes of the useful English-trained pair, Large Action and Mysilv, in the line-up. They, like their Irish counterparts, had reputations for indomitable courage and endurance.

Expectations were high as the precocious mare, Mysilv, set off at a scorching, lung-bursting pace, attempting in her usual audacious fashion to gallop the opposition into the ground. Charlie Swan had Danoli hard on her heels, tracking her closely in case she built up a lead that would require radar to find her. He gave the horse his head approaching the second last and Danoli cruised effortlessly to the front, jumping it like a buck. The gallant Mysilv, vainly attempting to stay on terms, hit the hurdle and crashed out of the race.

Danoli's devastating injection of pace left Large Action and Dorans Pride trailing, but the race was far from over. The Paddy Mullins-trained Boro Eight, a 33-1 outsider, loomed up on the outside and laid down a formidable challenge. Over the last and down the straight they fought neck and neck, the huge crowd roaring them on.

Boro Eight threatened again and again in the battle to the line but Danoli, who has the heart of a lion, refused to give ground. He ran on strongly to win by three-quarters of a length, with Large Action seven lengths away in third and Dorans Pride a distant fourth.

The beaten trainers were generous in their praise. 'Danoli's some horse,' Paddy Mullins told me. Paddy's a near-neighbour of mine from Goresbridge, just across the River Barrow on the Carlow-Kilkenny border. He became an Irish hero following his remarkable Champion Hurdle-Cheltenham Gold Cup double with Dawn Run, and I've yet to meet a shrewder judge.

Oliver Sherwood, trainer of third-placed Large Action, was similarly gracious. 'We were beaten by a better horse,' he said. 'Danoli is absolutely super.' And Michael Hourigan – we'd briefly crossed swords after Danoli's victory in the Sun Alliance – admitted: 'No excuses. Danoli was by far the better horse on the day.' I was grateful to them all, but I wonder what they'd have said if they'd realised that Danoli's epic victory had been achieved with a broken leg?

The roar that went up as we made our way to the unsaddling enclosure was deafening. It was as if the whole of County Carlow had moved to Aintree. Everybody wanted to pat me on the back, shake my hand or crush my bones with bear-hugs. Still more wanted to hoist me high on their shoulders. And I could imagine the people at home dancing jigs of joy in front of their TV sets. Yet it wasn't just the Irish who were celebrating. I sensed the British, too, had taken Danoli to their hearts, for they joined in the acclaim in their thousands.

This unique occasion should have come a close second to the winning of the Sun Alliance as the greatest moment of my life. But, sadly, my heart wasn't in it. I felt uneasy inside; my stomach was beginning to churn. At the back of it all was my concern for Danoli. Charlie Swan was at first spellbound by the joy of it all; but, underneath, he, too, was worried that the horse might have been injured. He'd thought, there was something different about Danoli, but hadn't been able to put his finger on it. He said the horse had hung all the way up the straight, as if feeling an injury; but the fact he pinged the last two hurdles and got the better of Boro Eight on the run-in suggested there was nothing seriously amiss. Maybe a bit of soreness in one of his legs due to the firmness of the ground, but that was all. Or so we thought.

But now, amid the bustle and the back-slapping, I was becoming anxious. I'd grown so close to Danoli that I could pick up the signals he was sending. Something was wrong. I knew it. I couldn't get out of the winner's enclosure quickly enough. I wanted to be with Danoli, the horse who, along with my family, meant almost as much to me as life itself. I wanted to examine him and speak to the vets, to satisfy myself that all was well. And, if necessary, to comfort him.

I tore myself free from the sea of well-wishers not a moment too soon, for Danoli was in distress when I reached him. I thought it must be one of his tendons. Yet as I took the boots off, I couldn't believe it: there was nothing wrong with them. They were as straight as could be.

But the minute the boot on his near-fore came off, you could see it swelling up. It was like a balloon being inflated. The sweat just pumped through the horse and he trembled all over with the pain. God alone knows how he'd managed to finish the race, let alone win it. The vets were filled with compassion. They injected him straight away to kill the pain and bandaged him up well. It was all they could do. There was obviously a serious problem with the leg. We had to find out just how serious.

The driver backed the horse ambulance into the little narrow corridor to save Danoli walking farther than necessary. There was only an inch or two's leeway either side and it was the most amazing piece of manoeuvring I'd seen. He and the vets hardly let the horse take a step; I don't know how they did it. Then came that incredible drive to Leahurst. Under normal circumstances I'd have felt like royalty. As it was, there was a deep despondency hanging over me. It turned to despair when I was shown the X-rays: Danoli had cracked the fetlock joint between the cannon bone and long pastern. The official terminology went like this: 'Radiography revealed a complete, displaced parasagittal fracture of the lateral condyle of the cannon bone with fragmentation of the articular margins.' Just as I'd suspected!

This was a terrible injury, in whatever language it was couched, and the upshot was that the leg would have to be pinned together with screws. We were told it would be a long job and that there was no guarantee the operation would be successful.

They couldn't do anything for Danoli there and then, apart from making him comfortable. He'd have to be stabilised and prepared for surgery and we learned that the operation couldn't be performed until the following Monday, so it was pointless staying. I hated the thought of leaving him, but there was clearly no choice. Much as I'd like to have taken him home to Ireland, he wouldn't have managed the journey.

I was at rock-bottom when I said goodbye. It was like leaving a close member of the family in the care of total strangers and not knowing when you'd see them again. However, at the same time, I knew that he couldn't have been in better hands.

There was a lump in my throat and tears in my eyes as I gave Danoli a hug and reassured him that all would be well. I'm convinced he understood me. I prayed later that he wouldn't suffer and that eventually he'd make a complete recovery. It required a giant act of faith. The state his leg was in, you wouldn't have given tuppence for his chances.

I realise full well that my affection for Danoli goes way beyond any normal racehorse-trainer relationship. I not only love this horse with all my heart, but I'm also deeply in awe of him. He'd been so brave that day, braver than anyone will ever know, and had paid a heavy price. Maybe the ultimate price. But that's his nature: he'd rather die than lose a race he has a chance of winning.

Nobody knows for certain when he broke the leg. For what it's worth, I believe it happened when he made that huge salmon-leap at the second last. It takes some believing that any horse could have possessed the courage to run on like he did; and remember, he wasn't facing 'selling platers : we're talking of the finest hurdlers in the British Isles. To have seen them off while racing on only three legs and racked with searing pain required a triumph of the spirit given to the very few and the very special.

In fact, he'd been too brave for his own good. The fairy-tale looked as if it was over.

WE'D long since missed the plane to Ireland, so we got a taxi back to the racecourse and linked up with one of the horseboxes leaving the track for the ferry. The journey home took twelve hours in all and it seemed endless. Few words were spoken. I was broken up inside. It's hard to believe you could win a big race at Aintree and not be in the mood to celebrate, even if, in my case, it would have been with a soft drink. It was eight o'clock the next morning when we finally arrived home, worn out and worried stiff.

We rang Leahurst later that day and they gave us the full rundown on the horse. The veterinary surgeon we spoke to was Dr Chris Riggs, a man with a string of letters after his name longer than a line full of washing. He was Head of the Equine Division and hadn't been there the day before, when Danoli was brought in. But he and his team were exceptionally helpful and went out of their way to explain it all to us.

They'd been snowed under with calls from the public asking after the welfare of the horse. Because of the Grand National – won that year by Jenny Pitman's Royal Athlete – few people at the meeting had realised Danoli was in trouble. It was only the following day, when the Sunday papers hit the streets, that the full story emerged. The hospital authorities said the phones hadn't stopped ringing. They'd never experienced anything like it before. There were reporters pacing around outside the gate and camera lads looking to get in and take photos of the horse. People started sending postcards addressed simply: 'Danoli, Liverpool'.

AT ten o'clock on the Monday morning, Danoli was given a general anaesthetic and moved to the operating theatre. Chris Riggs performed the operation in tandem with his boss, Professor Barrie Edwards, Head of the Department of Veterinary Clinical Science and Animal Husbandry. It took four hours and involved an open reduction of the fracture followed by the insertion of two orthopaedic screws. An arthrotomy was performed on the fetlock joint, to remove multiple bone chips and to ensure the joint surfaces were accurately aligned. The team's main concern was the severe erosion of the cartilage covering the bones of the joint, which greatly increased the risk of osteoarthritis setting in. Following the operation, a temporary cast was applied to the limb to protect the fracture while he regained his feet.

According to Chris Riggs, Danoli made an excellent recovery from the anaesthetic and stood calmly enough on the leg. When he left the operating theatre, he found his message clip bulging with telephone enquiries from the racing correspondents of just about every newspaper in Britain and Ireland.

Post-operative radiography confirmed that the fracture had been considerably reduced and had remained stable while Danoli recovered from the anaesthetic. The cast was later removed and replaced with a large bandage. Danoli appeared to be comfortable on the limb and happy to walk on it. The hospital confirmed he was an excellent patient, maintaining 'a calm and gentle demeanour when he was receiving injections and while his bandages were being changed'. Chris Riggs said he felt the surgery had been a success, but a lot could still go wrong and everything depended on how the joint progressed from there. If it remained free from infection and there were no other problems, he'd be cautiously optimistic.

Whether the leg would ever be sound enough for the horse to race again was another matter entirely.

2

Getting Going and Tipping Around

DANOLI'S injury and hospitalisation coincided with the beginning of jump racing's close season here in Ireland and across the water in England. It's the time of year when the more fortunate horses are turned out into the fields by their owners and Danoli would normally have been one of them. He spends the summers frolicking around and generally enjoying himself on Danny O'Neill's farm.

The yard virtually closes down until the autumn, but there's always plenty to do. The horses still have to be fed and cleaned and exercised, the stables have to be mucked out daily and there are a hundred and one other things to contend with, like playing catch-up on jobs that we never have time to do during the busy winter season.

This seems as good a time as any, then, to tell you something about my training establishment and my background and the events that led up to my becoming trainer of a racehorse who has lit up my life, and the lives of the countless thousands who have seen him in action at the racetracks or watched him on TV.

I was brought up in the faith of my forebears and I'm sure you're all familiar with the saying, 'Once a Catholic, always a Catholic'. True enough, I've never paid much attention to other creeds or cults. That doesn't mean to say I don't respect them or believe that their followers aren't good and decent people. It's just that I'm happy enough with my own religion and have never had the time or the inclination to study anything else.

It follows, then, that I know little about reincarnation, apart from bits I've heard. But, as I understand it, we die and return to earth several times until we become perfect beings. Then there's no need to come back any more. Apparently the belief is that each time we return, we get to choose our own parents, according to the lessons we have to learn. If it's true – the bit about the parents, I mean – then all I can say is that I made a fair fine job of choosing mine.

For I owe a lot to my dad, Tom, and my mother Mary, née Nolan. They're both gone now, but in their own way they moulded and shaped me and gave me character. And I like to think they gave me a decent upbringing. They were just ordinary country people who lived off the land and had good values which they passed on to me and to my brothers John, Jim, Pat and Ger and my sister Mary. I hope and pray I never let them down.

They owned the house and 62-acre farm where I now live with my wife, Goretti, and our family. It's in a tiny hamlet called Aughabeg on the outskirts of Bagenalstown in County Carlow, some seventy miles south of Dublin. I wouldn't describe it as being particularly remote, but the house and farm are tucked well away from the road and this presents a problem for first time visitors. For the most part they are Danoli fans on a pilgrimage and they have a rare old time finding us. They come from far and wide and very often land on us without notice. They can also arrive at the most inconvenient of times, generally when we're at our busiest. But we always do our best for them because, such is the horse's popularity, they think they own him. Danny O'Neill and ourselves are happy enough to go along with that, as in a sense they do. It's why he's called the People's Champion.

The house is the very one in which I grew up, but you wouldn't know the farm. Instead of cattle we now have horses; and instead of fields of corn and hay and the like we have two all-weather gallops, one wood-chip and the other sand. We've four separate stable blocks that house Danoli and the other 40 or so horses in training here, and just recently we installed a £15,000 eight-unit horse-walker. So you see, we may be tucked away in a rural part of Ireland, but we're keeping up with all the latest equipment and technology. There's a new millennium round the corner and we'll be giving the big boys a run for their money.

That doesn't mean we're burying the past. Far from it, for if there's one aspect of modern-day living that I can happily do without, it's hi-tec security. We've none of that stuff here at Aughabeg. My security is an old-fashioned shotgun and I wouldn't be afraid to use it if I found someone snooping around without permission. We used to keep it for foxes and rabbits and, when we had crops, for frightening off the crows. It's a better deterrent than any burglar alarm.

People might wonder how a man can live all his life in the same three-bedroom house and spend all his working days on the same old piece of land. But I wouldn't swap it for Buckingham Palace, or the grounds that surround it. For a start, the Queen doesn't have the view of the Blackstairs Mountains – and, beyond them, Mount Leinster – that greet me every morning of my working day. You couldn't put a price on that. This place is a large part of me; it's in my blood and everything I achieve in racing will have its beginning here. Who knows, I might even succeed in putting Aughabeg on the map – literally – because it isn't at the moment. Then people would have no trouble finding us.

We all live in the present and we all have aims for the future – but our links are with the past. And in my view, we shouldn't be in too big a hurry to forget them. When I get a moment at the end of a busy day, I sometimes think back to my childhood. It was in the late forties and the fifties and sixties that I was growing up on the farm and I like to remind myself how different things were then.

I was born third in line in the Foley dynasty. That was on 5 November 1946, which makes me 51. John's knocking on now at 54 and Jim's not far behind at 53. Pat's 49, Mary's 47 and Ger's the baby at 45. They all live locally, apart from Jim. He's based in Toronto and works for a Canadian oil company.

We were a happy family, content and close-knit. My mother was brought up only five miles from here and her people were all mad keen on racing – particularly a young brother, whose every waking hour was consumed by horses and greyhounds. My dad, too, was daft on the sport. So I suppose racing, or the love of it, runs right through our veins.

I described my parents as 'ordinary' and by that I meant they never thought of themselves as being grand. In fact, when I think about it, they were really quite extraordinary – especially my mother, who was a great lady in every way and at camogie, the female version of hurling. She played with the local Myshall Blues and was elected both for the county, Carlow, and the province, Leinster. In 1934, she won a solid silver Leinster medal.

When she finished playing, she maintained her links by becoming a club administrator. She was always present whenever I played for Naomh Eoin (Saint John), or when the Myshall Camogie Club was in action. I can't remember her missing a match. She'd attend all the senior hurling finals and was a familiar figure in the stand at Dr Cullen Park. Well-known and much-loved, her death in 1995 was a sad loss for us all. I suppose I inherited her passion for sport and certainly her competitive spirit. I like to think so, because to her no challenge was too great.

Each year a sportsman or woman is elected by the local GAA to the County Carlow Hall of Fame and Mam was given that honour shortly after her death. The great thing is that she was with us through the early Danoli years and lived to see his successes in the Sun Alliance Hurdle and the Martell Aintree Hurdle. She was thrilled to bits but, to my regret, my father, who died in 1980, was no longer around. He'd have been so proud.

Dad was a fan of all kinds of sports, including racing and football. And, of course, hurling; he had little choice there! He liked nothing better than going to the tracks to watch the dogs and horses run. He loved the horses more than anything, but never got as far as owning one.

I went to the local national schools, first to St Finian's at Garryhill and from there to Ballinkillen. I must be honest and admit that I was never much good at school. Either I couldn't get on with it or it couldn't get on with me. I've never quite worked out which. But times were harder in those days – a whole lot harder.

I had to walk three-and-a-half miles to school and back and there was a fair bit of work to be done on the farm. Nowadays everything's changed. The children get picked up by busse or car sand lots of them stay in education till they're 25 or more. Then they find they can never turn their hands to anything.

At least we went out and worked. We didn't mind what we did to earn a bob or two – picking the potatoes and anything we could get hold of. If we got paid some money we were allowed to keep it and that would encourage us to work. But the young people growing up today aren't interested – they just won't do it. That's the way it is.

My parents were never what you'd call strict. In fact they were easy to get along with because of their interest in sport; it was a common thread that bound the family together. All the young lads were into one sport or another and school never rated as much of an attraction. It's a wonder any of us can even read or write. We took part in every kind of sport: football, hurling, handball, tug of war, darts. You name it, we played it. School always happened to come a poor second to sport.

Each evening, I worked on the farm but there'd be homework to do and it couldn't be missed. The result was that I usually ended up rushing it. I can't pretend it was something I ever enjoyed.

It was a busy life, working the land, and a tough one. We had dairy cows and beef cattle and there was tillage, too. Mixed farming is what you'd call it. At that time there was no such thing as slatted houses. The cattle were out and we had to take the feed to them, and do the milking. Most days we'd beaver away till gone nine at night, but I wasn't one for watching the clock and I'm the same now. I wasn't made to do it or even asked – I just chipped in and helped, the same as everyone else.

I grew older and left school, but at that point I had no ambition to go into racing. None whatsoever. For one thing, it was above us at that stage; you had to have a lot of money and we didn't. However, I was always interested in horses and after a few years of working and tipping around, I got money enough to buy one. It was an Irish draught – a non-thoroughbred of the type they breed show-jumpers from. I bred some nice foals from her and used to love watching them running around the field. The money in it wasn't great, but it was a good experience and I learned a bit about how to handle horses. From there I hoped to graduate to thoroughbreds but, as things turned out, that wouldn't be for a few years yet. Not, in fact, until after I was married.

I can tell you for certain that once you own a horse, you're hooked. You start becoming involved and it's difficult to get it out of your system. You try to find more money to keep going and that's how it continues. I used to go to the races with my dad and

I suppose that's where the seed was sown. I liked the excitement of it all. I got to thinking, 'Wouldn't it be nice to have a horse you could win a race with?'

However, I was still young and sport was the big thing in my life. I'd played lots of Gaelic football for the schools and the local teams – including Minor and Under-21 for the County League – and we'd won plenty of trophies. Nobody played much soccer in those days – not in Carlow, anyway. Jack Charlton hadn't been invented.

It was through playing football that I met up with Goretti Fox. Goretti was actually her middle name; her first, Maria, got dropped somewhere along the line. Goretti lived about 15 miles away in Myshall, where Danny O'Neill has his farm, and she had brothers playing football and hurling; in fact, we were all playing together. Nearly everyone in Myshall was supporting Naomh Eoin, because they hadn't won a thing since 1938. When I was playing for them it was 1968 and I was coming up for 22. They had a big following – so big it was nearly like Danoli's, which is really something when you consider it'd been 30 years or so since they'd last got their hands on a trophy.

For five or six years at that time there was tremendous excitement around Myshall, because from winning nothing Naomh Eoin started winning almost everything. They won Intermediate and they won Senior and Junior. They'd maybe get beaten in the Senior football, but go on to win the Senior hurling, and it kind of went on like that. The passions and emotions these games aroused were really something. The supporters used to work themselves into a frenzy and so did the players. I can't pretend I was an angel myself, either. I wasn't afraid of losing my temper and I'd never back down, even if the fellah was 6ft 5in. There were a few skirmishes but nothing serious. I think these days they'd call it handbags at five paces. We won stacks and stacks of medals, but I've no idea where any of them are now.

From that day to this, Naomh Eoin has been rated one of the top teams in the county. The Senior side won the Carlow Championship six years in a row. It's funny how fortunes change.

Goretti used to come to watch her brothers play and there were local dances, too. We went steady for three or four years and got married in 1974, when she moved in here with me and my parents. By that time, the rest of the family had married and moved out. I was the only one left.

We were farming for a good three years. Then along came Sharon and Adrienne in fairly quick succession, which meant Goretti had her hands full. The arrival of little Goretti and a son, Patrick, would complete the family, but that was still some way down the road.

I was doing all the work on the farm and it was tough making ends meet. My father had retired and although he still helped out a bit, the farming was mine and I was responsible for it. I was doing a piece of hire work as well, trying to make money by working for other people. It was hard and we never seemed to be getting any better off. We were always struggling.

Then we started in at the horses. We had no stables as such but I quickly set to work, building the lower ones first. They weren't great but at the time they were good enough. Then, we started getting a few extra horses and I built five more along the other side. I did most of the labouring myself. I could do block-work and building was something I liked. Which was just as well, because we couldn't afford to have it done.

After we'd been going a good few years, we found we were still no better off. However, we were getting that little piece more to do with the horses; and the more we got involved with them, the more difficult it became to cope with the farming. At that stage we started cutting back on the farm work and so it went on, until eventually we were able to phase it out altogether. But that wasn't until relatively recently.

The first thoroughbred I bought was called Ulay and cost £500. She was good, but I didn't train her myself. She got hurt and broke down badly and I kept her for breeding.

I decided then to team up with my brother Pat, who's a builder, and Tom Donohue, who keeps a few horses of his own and runs a machine hire place in Milltown, just across the way. Between us we bought a Deep Run mare called December Run, who, as I recall, cost £2,000. We broke her and got her going and she seemed fairly promising. She was put with a trainer but, unfortunately, she got hurt and we decided to bring her home. We gave her to another trainer; he did a good job all right and in her first race she finished fifth. But she broke down fairly badly then and that was that. We had her leg pinfired, brought her back and decided we'd start working on her ourselves.

At the time, I was getting a good few horses in and was desperately in need of an all-weather track. There was an old field up near the house which we used to turn to hay or corn and the like, and it was just about big enough for a three-furlong gallop. That was the minimum distance I'd require, but earth-moving equipment needed to be hired and an efficient drainage system laid. It was a pricey operation and, handy as I was, I couldn't possibly do the work myself. But I knew a man who could. In fact, I knew two men.

Pat and Tom Donohue between them possessed the know-how and the machinery and they duly installed a wood-chip gallop that was to prove an absolute godsend. As I would now be housing, feeding and training December Run, we came to a right good agreement over the cost. My Latin's a bit rusty but a *quid pro quo*, I think, is what you'd call it.

It was around this time that Padraic (Padge) Gill, a local jockey, came on the scene. The three of us went to see him and asked if he'd ride December Run in a schooling piece of work. It was shortly before Cheltenham and there were a number of Festival horses being put through their paces. I said to Padge, 'Go out and do whatever you think should be done with her – you know, just to see what she's made of.'

So Padge started her out at the back of the field. He moved to the front with her and then he took her near to the back again. Despite going backwards and forwards like this, she won the piece of work nice and easy. Padge told me afterwards: 'This one is a very, very good mare.' We decided to run her in a race in Leopardstown, where she finished third, but she broke down afterwards and never recovered.

That set me back a good bit and it got me thinking about breeding from Ulay. At the time Deep Run was going well at stud, and I liked him as a sire because I'd thought quite a bit of December Run. He was standing at the Coolmore Stud and the fee of £3,500 reflected how highly he was rated as a stallion. So I scraped together the money and brought Ulay to Deep Run to get her in foal. Thankfully she got a real nice filly which we called Deep Endeavour, and things started to take off from there. I trained her myself and won a couple of races with her.

But I'm getting a bit ahead of myself. The very first horse I trained to win was called Rua Batric. Padge Gill was the means of getting her for me because she was owned by a friend of his, Paddy Bennett, a Wexford man who had a furniture store, an aluminium window company and a pub and, as such, didn't have to worry where his next meal was coming from.

Padge asked him if he wanted Rua Batric trained. Begorrah, yer man agreed to it and we began to train her. Now Paddy, who was in his early fifties, was the type who wouldn't mind a gamble, so I ran Rua Batric in a race at Gowran, our local track. I'm not sure where she finished – I think it was third or fourth – and I said to him, 'This one is in at Tramore and she'll win in Tramore.'

She was a filly who didn't want ground too soft and, of course, it spilt the whole day and night before the race. We went down to

Tramore and the ground was very, very soft, and I said to Paddy, 'I still think she'll win it.' We saddled up the filly and off she went to the start.

Coming back up, Paddy was there and I asked him, 'Well, did you put a good few pounds on her?' He muttered something about a monkey and I didn't get him.

I came back up on to the stand, then, to watch the race and there was a lad standing nearby. I said to him, 'Is a monkey £500?'

And he said, 'Yeah.' I didn't take any more notice and that was grand, anyhow, because the filly won at 6-1.

Next day the farriers were at the farm when who walked in but Paddy Bennett.

I said to him, 'Paddy, if you like you can tell me to mind me own business, but when I said yesterday to you about backing the filly, what did you tell me you'd do? Have a monkey on her or what?'

'Oh no,' he says, 'I had five-and-a-half monkeys on her.'

Well, the boys got such a fear they all nearly dropped their cups. And I said to him, 'Begod, Paddy, if I'd known that, I'd have been caught for coming home before the races, for I wouldn't have been there.'

So that was the way with Rua Batric. She ran a couple of times afterwards, but she was a filly who was prone to different things going wrong, In the end we decided there was no point keeping going with her and I then got a few different horses from Roly Kidd - horses that weren't good feeders or that weren't going too well for other trainers.

Roly was a big farmer from a place called Slyguff, on the way out to Goresbridge, and we were lucky enough with him. We won two bumpers with one of his horses, Young Bavard. Then Padge Gill rode him in his first hurdle race for me and he won that, too. He was later sold and ended up running in England. Funnily enough, it was the only horse Padge rode for me in a race for he got hurt shortly afterwards and the doctors wouldn't let him ride again. He'd suffered a lot of injuries during racing and while he wasn't champion, he was up among the top four or five jockeys at the time. He was a very obliging lad and I think if he'd been able to stay riding a few years longer, it would have made a great difference to me.

I could ask anything of him. If he said a horse was going well or was fairly useful, well, you could listen to Padge because he knew what he was talking about. We had to go the hard road then without him. We had no one else to turn to and we had to start making it on our own. Padge was living in Gowran; and although he couldn't ride for us any more, and we didn't see nearly so much of him, he was able to give us the odd bit of advice. He was always helpful and honest. He'd never try and cod you in any way or lead you on. Goretti says we'd have been nothing without him and maybe that's true; what I know for sure is that things would have been a whole lot tougher.

Padge has started work for Red Mills, the horse-feed manufacturers, so we see him from time to time when he comes to take our order. It gives us the chance to chat and go back over old times.

> 'The first time I set eyes on Tom was when he, his brother Pat and Tom Donohue drove into my yard one evening and asked if I'd ride out December Run. I said, 'Fine, I will.' That was about 14 years ago and it was the beginning of a really good relationship with Tom. Shortly afterwards he hurt his back and I used to go over and ride a good few mornings. It just went on from there. I did a lot of his riding out and broke in a good few horses for him around that time.
>
> 'When I first met Tom, he didn't know a big lot about the workings of racing with regard to handicaps. He wasn't used to dealing with that type of thing, but he had a good feel for

the game and a great way with horses – a kind of empathy with them. I was a freelance at the time and riding out for a lot of people. So I could tell he was doing a great job.

'I had a fall from a horse called Camflower in a race at Gowran Park in 1990 and got broken up. I was paralysed for a while on the ground and they couldn't move me. I'd injured my back and it finished me as a jockey. I ended up with an enlarged ligament beside the spinal chord and the medics wouldn't give me back my licence. They said if I had the same type of fall again, I'd be paralysed for life. Sure, you always hear that, anyway. I'd been a jockey 19 years on the Flat and over the jumps and it's tough to be told you can never ride again.

'I rode 35 winners in 1988 and it was my best year ever. Yet two years later, at the age of 34, I was done for. My last winner was in the Thyestes at Gowran – once won by the mighty Arkle – on a well-known horse called Mweenish, trained in England by the late John Webber. So at least I went out on a high note.

'I don't go to many meetings now – just here at Gowran and occasionally to Punchestown. I ride out now and then for Tony Mullins, but I'm not allowed over the jumps. Just recently, on an impulse, I rode out for Tom one morning. I grabbed someone's gear, put it on and jumped on a horse. Just for old time's sake. I missed it all so much.'

We missed Padge, too, and it was the hard road ahead. Yet we pushed on and thanks be to God we never were short of horses. We had one that year belonging to Tom Donohue called Dorking, and we entered him in an event at Dundalk a few weeks before the big meeting in Galway. He ran a good race, and we thought he was well enough to produce the goods in Galway. So begorrah we all set off for the first day of the big meeting and he was 14-1. Tom

Donohue had a good few pounds on him and he won. I had him entered up in another race in Galway, but this one was over a mile and a half on the Flat. I thought he had enough speed for it and, thankfully, I was right. He won that race, too. So from there on we knew we were learning and there were more lads enquiring and giving us the opportunity of doing. We were running horses in good races at all the big meetings. Naas was known as the punter's graveyard but we were lucky enough – we won more races there than anywhere else – and Leopardstown was where we always found it hardest to win.

Until Danoli came along.

3

The Bone-setter Gets His Horse

ONE day Danny O'Neill, a celebrated bone-setter from these parts, asked me about buying a horse. I didn't take him seriously and did nothing about it.

We were family friends of some years' standing. Our fathers knew each other well and Danny's old fellah often came to our place for a game of cards. In those days there was no television and people gathered in each other's houses of a Sunday night for a few hands of poker and the like. Danny used to come, too – himself and the father. The father wouldn't have been great at driving the car and Danny used to chauffeur him. At that time he wasn't into the bone-setting. I won't say he knew nothing about it: he never had to know because it was his uncle who had the gift.

When the father died Danny took over the farm in Myshall. He got going in the bone-setting then, too, for his uncle convinced him he could do it and he also proved it to his own satisfaction. His reputation spread and people from all over began going to him.

So you see, I knew Danny fine well that time; and when we were playing the football, we often had to call on him. Players would get hurt and he'd fix them up.

It was on one of those occasions that he said to me, 'I was thinking of getting a horse. Will you get me a horse?'

And I replied, 'Yeah, definitely – no problem.'

I said to Goretti afterwards, 'Danny's looking for a horse but I wouldn't mind that. I bet there'll be no more about it.'

I don't know how long went by - possibly it was eight or nine months or more – before he said, 'You never did anything about getting me that horse!'

'Begod,' I said, 'if you really want a horse, I won't be long getting you one. There's a Goffs catalogue after just coming in and possibly the best thing to suit you is a filly. If you buy a gelding and something happens to him, he's no good to you. But a filly – at least if you go out and pay money for her and she breaks down and gives trouble that way, you can breed a foal out of her and you'll have something coming on.'

He said: 'I don't mind – I don't know the difference one way or the other. Go ahead.'

So I said: 'Right enough. We'll go up to the sales together and you can pay for her yourself.'

He answered: 'What would I go up for? I know nothing at all about it.'

And I just said: 'Come up - be there anyway. At least you'll see what she's costing and you'll know whether she's too dear or too cheap.'

It was the summer of 1991 and, anyhow, he agreed to go. I drove up to Kill in Kildare early on the morning of the sale. I wanted to have something picked out ready for him and I'd decided to have a really good look round. I had plenty of horses marked out in the catalogue and I went and looked at them all. Some were too small and some were this and some were that and there wasn't any of them in it that would suit.

From walking around everywhere and looking in over every door, I just happened to come to where Danoli stood. Of course, he wasn't named then. I stopped and said to myself, 'I'll go in and have a look at him.' He was a three-year-old bay gelding by that prolific sire, The Parson, out of a winning mare called Blaze Gold and I liked the cut of him. He had a good-looking, intelligent face and alert eyes. Everything else about him seemed to measure up, too. He was the perfect size for a future chaser – and he looked a fine stamp of a horse. A lot of nonsense is talked about perfect conformation and this, that and the other. The truth is that a lot of fantastic-looking horses turn out to be hopeless and with me, it's all down to instinct and feeling – I wouldn't try and tell you otherwise. If I knew which horses were going to turn out champions just by looking at them, I'd have a fleet of helicopters in the yard. Yet there was something about this fellah that I liked.

The owner and breeder was Willie Austin, a dairy farmer from Cloughjordan in Tipperary. I asked Willie to take out the horse and walk him and trot him around. I checked him over and liked him even more. I asked Willie what he wanted.

He said: 'The horse will make £10,000.'

I said: 'Well, we won't be paying that for him anyhow.'

Danny had never said to me beforehand: 'I'll spend such and such' and I'd never asked him, so it made it that little bit harder to bargain. Even when he arrived, we still didn't discuss price. I just said to him, 'There's not a decent mare in it, but there's a horse I like and I think you should buy him.' He didn't mind one way or the other, so I told him, 'Now we won't bid for him unless he goes on the market, because if he goes on the market he's here to be sold. And if he doesn't, God only know what way it'll be.'

In the event Danoli went into the ring, but the top bid was £5,800 and he was taken out unsold. So I went outside and had a punt with Willie Austin: 'In the long run, £7,000 is the price for the horse. If you don't want it, no problem – there'll be lot of horses in the Derby sale coming up in a week's time. We'll find something then.'

And that was that. He walked away and into the pub, and the wife was there and she was kind of anxious for him to sell. So I thought I'd better firm things up with Danny.

I said to him, 'Look it, will you pay £7,000 for the horse? I think he's worth it.' Danny said he would. So I sent one of the lads into the pub and Willie Austin came out.

I said to him, 'Do you want to sell the horse or not? If you don't it's all right, anyhow, but nobody else seems to want him. There's my name and number. If you want to sell, give me a ring. Because if not I'll go up to the Derby sales and buy one.'

Right, that was grand. The horse went home and we went home. Two days later the phone rang and Willie said he'd sell. We arranged out with Danny and he said he'd go down to Tipperary and collect the horse.

I said to Danny: 'Call Willie Austin now for good luck because the horse, there's nothing cheap about him. And there wouldn't be another like him in the Derby sales. You'll get a few hundred pound luck out of it anyhow.'

Danny phoned and yer man said he'd bring up the horse. Then he rang the next day and said, 'If you want the horse, you may come for it.'

Danny said he'd go because he was travelling down to Tipp one way or the other. So Danny took the box with him and brought back the horse. He said, 'I didn't get a whole lot of luck anyhow.'

I think £20 luck money is what he got. 'Anyway,' I said, 'it makes no odds, because I like the horse.'

A couple of different lads called in afterwards and looked at him in the stable. They hadn't too much good to say about him – he was too short and he was this, that and the other – and I just said, 'You won't be saying that when he wins his bumper first time out.' I was only hoping that would happen – it was a bit of bravado on my part.

So we started off and he seemed a nice horse right from day one. He did everything right, like a horse who wanted to go. It was a lad by the name of Martin Hallbrook who broke him; he was a Wexford man working in Jim Bolger's at the time. Danoli was coming along really, really nice, so Martin did a little piece with him, broke him and got him right. He came back over here, then, and we did a little bit more work with him before letting him out for the summer. He went to Danny's for a time and when he came back he was as fat as a pig. We started working hard on him and I was always saying to Danny, 'This is a nice horse, this is a nice horse.'

Before he was broken, I had a horse here belonging to a different lad, and a brother of Ferdy Murphy – I can't remember which brother, except it wasn't Declan – came to buy him. He had a car parked up above by the gate. He didn't like the other horse; I don't know whether it was too dear or what it was.

Anyhow, he's seen Danoli galloping down to the gate and he says: 'What's that?'

And I tell him: 'He's a horse we got the other day from a lad from Tipperary. We gave £7,000 for him.'

He says: 'Would you sell him?'

'Well, begod,' I says, 'I don't know. He belongs to another man.'

He answers: 'If he wants to sell him, tell him I'll double his money. I'll give him £14,000 for the horse.'

I rang Danny and he started to hum and ha. He didn't know what to do and he didn't make up his mind for six weeks. If he'd sold then, it would still have given him £1,000 a week profit. Finally he came up one day in the evening and said: 'Ah, I won't sell. I'll keep him – wait until he makes some good money and have a bit of craic with him. I won't sell him.'

That was grand, anyhow. We started to train the horse and he was going really, really well. I was so proud of him. I took him down to Bert Allen's in Courtown, Wexford. Bert was a big businessman. He was a major shareholder in Slaney Meats; he owned several hotels and had a lot of good horses. He used to own Granville Again, who went on to win the Champion Hurdle with Martin Pipe, so he knew a good animal when he saw one.

My intention was to give Danoli a change of scenery. It was worth the trip because it was right on the coast and we were able to use Bert's gallop by the beach. Afterwards, I walked Danoli in the sea and it did him a power of good. I said to Bert, 'This is a nice horse – this fellah will win first time out.' He was a man who wouldn't mind gambling a few pound but there was no more to it and I've no idea if Bert ever backed him.

We started preparing the horse for a two-mile bumper in Naas. We fancied his chances a lot but hadn't had enough horses through our hands to know how good they were. So it would have been easy enough to change our minds.

Danny was up a few days before we went to Naas and I said to him, 'Danny, is this horse for sale or is he not?'

He said, 'Why?'

I said: 'Well if he's for sale, put a price on him. And if you get it, sell him. Don't go putting a price on him and then, when you get it, start saying, "Oh no, I want so much." It's not lucky. If he's for sale, he's for sale. And if he's not, then don't price him.'

He said, 'Ah, I don't know.'

So off we went to Naas to run him. It was the last day of October 1992 and I remember it clearly. We were stabled in the top yard and began walking the horse round. He was fairly green. He'd never set foot on a course before and didn't have a clue.

There was a young lad there leading round another horse and I said to him, 'What's that?'

He said, 'Oh, he's in the bumper. He'll win the bumper.'

That was a blow to us. He pointed to Danoli and said, 'What's that?'

I said, 'He's a young horse – he was never on a racetrack before. He knows nothing.'

The bumper horses race last, which is why they're stabled in the top yard. They have to wait until the others go out before moving down to the lower stable yard to be saddled up. So we went down and there were a couple of lads there doing the rounds and talking about the horses. One of them says, 'Arthur Moore has a horse here, Atours, who'll walk the bumper. He ran in Naas ten days ago and Arthur got pulled in over him. But he's going to do the business here today.'

I thought, 'Well, that's that. There's no way we'll win this one.'

They were starting to build up against us, the ones that were going to beat us, so I just said to the lads who were with us, 'We needn't back this today – there's a couple of good horses here. Arthur Moore's is supposed to win this easy.'

Danoli ended up 16–1 and not one of us had a penny on him, bar little Goretti. She had £1 with her for sweets. Come the race, she went up and put down the £1. She was only eight at the time and she placed the bet with a bookie. It's a pity she didn't put it on with the Tote, because it paid out twice as much. But she wasn't to know and neither were we. We were pretty naive when it came to betting – still are, for that matter.

The race contained more drama than *EastEnders*. There was a stack of money for Atours, which wasn't surprising considering all the talk beforehand, and he went off the 11-10 favourite. His backers must have been counting their money just over a furlong out, judging by the noise they were making, but they changed their tune when the jockey aboard Atours, Humphrey Murphy, dropped his whip. The cheers turned swiftly to jeers as our man Padraig English, a 19-year-old amateur from Wexford, got Danoli up in a driving finish to score by a length.

It was Padraig's first winner. He had good cause to be delighted, but his celebrations were cut short when the stewards cautioned him for excessive use of the whip. Yet I wasn't the least bit angry with him. The horse had responded well to the whip and the fact the other jockey was having to push Atours out to the line made it look a hundred times worse for Padraig. From my point of view, Danoli had won his first race and I believe he'd have got up anyway. He wasn't marked or distressed and I was happy with the way things had gone. In fact, to use a soccer expression, I was over the moon and so was Goretti, now £16 the richer. I was as proud of her as I was of Danoli, because it must have taken real guts on her part to back the horse. When you're eight, £1 for sweets is not to be given up lightly.

The nice thing is that it was the Philip A. McCartan Memorial National Hunt Flat Race. Philip was a trainer from up around the Curragh; he got killed in a car crash and his father was one of the race sponsors. We got plaques that day for winning, which was lovely because it was our first race with Danoli. Danny O'Neill got one, Padraig English got one and I got one. I still have it.

The first words Danny said to me as we walked in were, 'No way is the horse for sale.'

I said, 'That's grand, anyhow.'

He was as white as white could be. He couldn't talk for about three days. It was his first time and I'd explained to him that if the horse won a race, it'd be very hard to describe the feeling you'd have. There was no bother because he wasn't able to talk, never mind describe his feelings. The little one was crowing all the way home because she was after backing a 16–1 winner. We'd all been talking on the way up about the odds we'd get and yet she was the only one to have put the money down.

The taste of victory was something to savour but, sadly, it didn't last. One day you're walking on air and the next you're back down to earth with a bump. Danoli, we discovered, was suffering from sore shins and we had to go to the river with him and do different things to try and get him right. He wouldn't run again for three months, in fact not until the end of January 1993.

But thoughts of how good he might become – how bright his star would shine – kept us feeling snug and warm over Christmas.

4

We Say 'No' to Charlie (Haughey, That Is)

THE festivities over and Danoli's shins cured, we could anticipate 1993 being a great year. Our first outing was a return to Naas at the end of January for the Irish National Bookmakers Flat Race over two miles and three furlongs. There was a horse in it, of Tipperary trainer Edward O'Grady, called Sea Gale. I heard it was going to run right away from us and we weren't going to win this race, either. There was another hotshot in it, too, called Hotel Minella, about whom there'd been an awful lot of talk. This was said to be really useful and it was to be ridden by Aidan O'Brien, who has since made such a tremendous impact as a trainer.

Danoli ended up 10–1 that day and this time they all had a little bit on, which was just as well because he won as he liked. No problems this time with whips or stewards – no dispute about the best horse in the race. Danoli coasted home by a very comfortable four lengths from Sea Gale, the 9-10 favourite, with Hotel

Minella another half-length back in third.

The race was a qualifier for the INB Flat Race Final the following month at Punchestown – a £7,000 event. Aidan O'Brien said he'd beat us at Punchestown because it was an easier track and a three-furlongs shorter trip. But we had still to decide between going there or to Cheltenham in March for the Festival bumper. I decided we wouldn't go for both.

Danny was no help. 'Well, I don't know,' he shrugged. 'That's what you're there for. It's for you to decide.'

I said: 'I'd rather go to Punchestown because I can put the horse in the box, drive there and drive back home – no problem. Maybe this horse won't travel well to Cheltenham. And once we're there, one lad will be saying the ground is grand and another will be saying it's firm and we'll end up running him either way. If it's firm, he might get sore shins and never be any good again. Whereas with Punchestown, we can go up and check the ground before we go.'

Danny said: 'If you want to go to Punchestown, go to Punchestown.'

I said: 'Right, then. That's settled. We're going to Punchestown.'

So I entered Danoli in the race and began preparing him; but thing were moving fast – so fast that I wasn't even sure he'd be running. There was big money being offered for the horse and plenty of people willing to pay it. Trainer John Mulhern was one of them. The talk was that he wanted to buy Danoli for his father-in-law, Charlie Haughey, the former Taoiseach. John sent a man here to see if he was for sale. The answer was 'No'. He said if we were ever going to sell, to let him know. He reckoned the horse would come up the finishing straight at Punchestown on his own and he was right.

Padraig English got to work on Danoli half a mile out and he drew away impressively to win by nine lengths from the useful Diplomatic, with Hotel Minella again finishing third – this time a distant 14 lengths adrift. I wonder what Aidan O'Brien thought in view of his comment that he'd beat us over this easy two miles. He'd have needed binoculars to get a sighting of Danoli from where he was.

Danoli had been made 5-2 favourite, which proved that the racing world was beginning to sit up and take notice. He simply walked away from everything else in the race as if they were standing still. And that was a real hot race. If people hadn't know it before, they knew it now: Danoli was a serious racehorse.

The pressure mounted for us to enter him for the Guinness Festival bumper at Cheltenham. We resisted the temptation but got plenty of stick because of it. There were comments in one or two newspapers – and to us personally – that we didn't deserve to have a good horse like Danoli if we were afraid to go to Cheltenham with him. I didn't care. I said, 'The horse will be out in the field tomorrow. I hate when you let out a horse and there's something wrong with him. He might have injured himself at Cheltenham. As it is he's sound and fresh as a daisy.'

After the summer break, we brought Danoli back and prepared him for hurdling. The first consideration was the choice of jockey. Padraig English, being an amateur, could no longer be considered and we decided we needed a big-name professional to partner Danoli in all his races. So we went for Charlie Swan, the champion. Charlie, of course, knew all about the horse and jumped at the chance.

We entered Danoli in a race in Punchestown but he got sore heels and some puffiness came into one of his hind legs. It was a bit of an infection and I decided I wouldn't run him. You wouldn't believe the kerfuffle that caused – the horse was broken up, he'd never run again and all the rest of it. I was beginning to learn that racing is always rife with rumour.

Time slipped by – I suppose a month or so – and a race came up at Fairyhouse, the Curragha Maiden Hurdle. We got Charlie to ride and we fancied Danoli strongly, as he'd taken really well to jumping at home. We'd rigged up a few hurdles here and from the very first day he went out, he jumped them, no problem. He won okay at Fairyhouse but not impressively to my mind. Charlie must have wondered what all the fuss was about. He probably thought, 'The horse isn't as good as they're trying to make out.'

The bookies had sent him off a 4-6 shot and he led from the start to beat Fambo Lad a handy four-and-a-half lengths. Michael Clower in *The Sporting Life* called Danoli's performance 'convincing' and rated it 'a pretty fluent hurdling display'. What's more, he named Danoli as the star of the show. Now Michael's job as a reporter is to describe the action as he sees it and comment accordingly, but trainers like me view things differently. We seek perfection from our horses and anything less can make us talk down a performance that to others might seem perfectly decent. Or even brilliant. I think that's the case here. After Danoli's runaway win at Punchestown and the way he'd been flying at home, I'd expected him to set the world alight in his first run over hurdles – especially in a modest field. To anybody else, the fact that he not only won but left the other 15 for dead would be rated a decent jumping debut.

My faith in Danoli remained as strong as ever. I had no doubts that he'd go right to the top as a hurdler and, eventually, a chaser. I had a star in the making and there was no horse in the country to touch him.

Two likely-looking races were coming up at Punchestown – the Morgiana Hurdle and the Ballycaghan Hurdle. So I took a chance and entered Danoli in both. Charlie Swan, who was contracted to Edward O'Grady, said he'd ride Danoli in the Morgiana because Edward's horse, Sound Man, was in the Ballycaghan.

Sound Man was potentially a serious horse. He was after winning his bumpers and in time would develop into a top two-mile chaser. Maybe my pride had the better of me, but I got to wondering what Charlie might do if the two horses were in the same race. So in the wind-up, I put Danoli into the Ballycaghan Hurdle. Charlie said he'd no choice but to ride Sound Man, which meant I'd have to find a different jockey. I booked Tommy Treacy to ride Danoli and they pulled Sound Man out of the race. Apparently, he'd developed an injury.

Danoli won in style to stretch his unbeaten run to five, trouncing the smart What A Question by four lengths. He deserved credit because he'd struck his face against a gate going out on the course. He gave himself quite a bang, for there was blood all over his mouth. This display of bravery was a sure sign of things to come.

Once again Danoli had been sent off an odds-on favourite, this time at 8-11, and nobody stout-hearted enough to back him at that skinny price had any worries. It was Tommy Treacy's 25th win and we kept him on board for Danoli's final outing of 1993 – the 1st Choice Novice Hurdle, to be run at Leopardstown two days after Christmas.

We'd hoped to end the year on a high, but everything that could go wrong did go wrong. On the way up to Leopardstown, the car towing the horsebox broke down. Luckily Jessica Harrington – who trains at Moone in Kildare – was passing in her horse lorry and I hailed her down. We loaded Danoli aboard but he'd never travelled in a lorry before and, of course, he panicked. Jim Treacy – Tommy's dad – climbed into the back to try and calm him but he worked himself into a right old state. Nevertheless, we decided to let him take his chance.

Danoli was forced to make the running and the pace was nowhere near fast enough. It wasn't Tommy's fault; it's just that Danoli doesn't always go a strong gallop when he's out on his own. He likes a bit of company and he didn't get it that day. Minella Lad, a confirmed stayer, was expected to blaze a trail but his rider, Trevor Horgan, let Danoli make it instead. This suited

John Shortt on Winter Belle, who sprinted clear to win by two lengths from Minella Lad. Danoli was a further half-length back in third.

Tommy was convinced Danoli would have won with a stronger pace and I agreed with him, but I reckoned the real reason for his defeat was that nightmare journey in the lorry. It was too much to expect him to run up to his best after using up so much nervous energy. I should have pulled him out, but hindsight is a wonderful thing and I wouldn't have been thinking that if he'd won. The bottom line was that the horse got beaten and it was no good us shedding any tears.

Danoli had lost his unbeaten record but knowing the reason why only confirmed our opinion that we had a potential champion on our hands. The places to prove it were Cheltenham and Aintree – and they were our targets for 1994. Some people thought his bubble had burst, but I didn't mind in the least. In a way, his defeat had eased the pressure on us and left us free to plan his build-up quietly.

The AIG Europe-sponsored Irish Champion Hurdle was coming up at Leopardstown towards the end of January and I was anxious to run him. It was a big race and would be by far his toughest test. I reckoned he'd learn a lot from it in the same way that I'd learned a lesson from Leopardstown the last time. And that was to steer clear of races where the jockeys might be messing about and saying, 'Let this one make it' or 'Let that one make it'. A valuable event like this – worth £30,000 to the winner – would likely be a true-run race and Danoli would have no problem in it. Nevertheless it still took a lot of thinking about because such a huge step up in class could break the heart of a novice.

Race entry was to close at twelve o'clock one Wednesday and we still hadn't our minds made up by ten o'clock. I knew well people would laugh at us if we put him into the Champion and so I went out to the lads in the yard and said: 'You know what I was thinking of doing? Putting Danoli in the Champion Hurdle.'

Danoli's work rider, Noel (Hammie) Hamilton, and a few of the others said: 'Sure. Go right ahead. He's up to it.'

I value the opinion of the lads in the yard. They know horses and they're good grafters – all of them. They work as a team and between them they're the best group of lads you could find anywhere. I must include my daughters, Sharon and Adrienne, here, because what applies to the lads applies to them also. Their commitment to the horses and their welfare is a hundred per cent. They're devoted to them to the extent that sometimes we worry that they're not going out to discos and such, like other young girls their age. But horses are their life and we leave it up to them. They're both fine riders and we've no worries on that score.

I'm not too puffed up with pride that I wouldn't ask Goretti's opinion or Sharon's or Adrienne's or any of the lads'. You can't possibly know it all; and sometimes you're too close to things to appreciate their importance. It's a day-to-day thing; we talk and discuss the whole time – not only matters concerning Danoli but all the horses in the yard.

Anyhow, the lads had confirmed my view and helped me make up my mind. I just needed that little bit of back-up – a push in the right direction. So I entered Danoli and thought I'd go up to Punchestown one day and give him a spin. I'd heard there were several Cheltenham-bound horses schooling that day and I was interested to see how Danoli would fare with them. I brought along another horse I had by the name of Ambitious Fellow, who was after winning his bumper and was a real good hurdler.

Tommy Treacy came up to ride Danoli but when I was above at Punchestown, who was in the yard but Tom Taaffe, son of the great Pat Taafe and a top-class jockey in his own right. I said to him: 'Tom, would you ride this other horse here? I want to school him and see what he's like. Set a real good pace, because if he's good enough he's going to Cheltenham.'

So Tom got up on Ambitious Fellow and he went a real good clip – 30 to 40 lengths in front of everything else in the school.

After they got back, he said to me: 'When we were over on the far side I looked round and your other lad, Danoli, moved up beside me with his mouth open and him running away. My God, that was faster than Cheltenham pace, the speed we travelled.' Tom knew Ambitious Fellow had gone well because they were so far in front of everything else. So you can imagine his surprise when Danoli flew past.

The school had been on the inside track. It wasn't very well marked out and Tommy Treacy had apparently gone part of the way on the wrong course. So the lads came back and started giving out about him and saying he was unable to ride the horse. Danny O'Neill wasn't there, but somebody went and told him Tommy took a different track altogether and jumped out over something that wasn't there, which was completely untrue.

Then, right out of the blue, Charlie Swan phoned. He came straight to the point. He said he'd ride Danoli in the Champion Hurdle because he thought he'd win it. It was a tremendous boost to hear him say that, especially as I'd been in two minds about running the horse. In addition, Charlie gave a commitment to ride him in all his future races, which was what I needed to hear. We couldn't go swapping jockey at every twist and turn.

Charlie had been after riding in the same piece of schooling work at Punchestown. He'd been aboard Shawiya, the 1993 Triumph Hurdle winner, and she was due to run in the Champion. As Charlie had got only a distant view of Danoli's backside, it brought home to him just how good the horse really was and what he was missing out on by not riding him.

I consulted Danny and he said: 'Well, if we can get the best, why not put him on it?'

I then had to tell Tommy he wouldn't be riding Danoli. And fair dos to him – he accepted it like a man, although he must have thought it had something to do with him taking the wrong course at Punchestown.

Charlie duly rode the horse at Leopardstown and the fact they finished a close-up second to Fortune And Fame proved that Danoli was capable not only of competing with the best but also of beating the best. It was certainly no disgrace to lose to the Michael W J Smurfit-owned, Dermot Weld-trained winner. Dermot had long held Fortune And Fame in the highest regard and as he said after the race: 'I told everybody as far back as November that this was a serious horse and he showed just how serious today.'

It had been a cracking contest that boiled up nicely just after the third from home, when Danoli and Shawiya went past the pace-setting Padre Mio. But Fortune And Fame, with Adrian Maguire on board, was simply cantering in behind and delivered his challenge at the second last. He swept into the lead and looked at one stage as if he'd run right away with the race. But I knew Danoli would battle and he didn't disappoint me. He stuck on really gamely to peg back Fortune and Fame all the way to the line, finally going under by just a length and a half, with Shawiya ten lengths back in third.

I was delighted with Danoli. It did my heart good to see the way he left Shawiya in the dust and chased home Fortune And Fame as if his very life depended on it. For a horse having only his fourth race over hurdles, I thought he'd covered himself in glory. Strictly speaking, he shouldn't have been in the same county as Fortune And Fame, let alone the same race. His price of 12-1 reflected that.

Charlie Swan reckoned we should run Danoli in the Sun Alliance Novices Hurdle at Cheltenham, a race he thought he'd have a great chance of winning. That would be in mid-March – seven weeks away - and I was eager to get another run into him before then. The Deloitte and Touche Hurdle back at

Leopardstown in February provided the perfect opportunity. It would put him absolutely spot-on for Cheltenham and leave me with an ideal four-week run-up to the Festival, during which time I'd be able to put the vital finishing touches to his preparation.

I was determined, too, to lay our Leopardstown bogey. I mentioned earlier that I'd never enjoyed much luck there in the past and the fact that Danoli's only two defeats had occurred at the famous old course just south of Dublin made me determined to put things right.

You try to look at things rationally, but it doesn't always work; emotions play a part and when you hardly ever win at a particular venue, you begin to feel jinxed. Most trainers have their favourite and least favourite courses and Leopardstown certainly wasn't top of my popularity list. We went back there hoping and praying for a change of fortune. But what happened? Danoli was lucky to escape injury when he slipped while being mounted and toppled over. Had the Leopardstown Curse struck again? I could surely have been forgiven for thinking it had, but, thankfully, horse and jockey were unscathed. Even so, I was left wondering what else could possibly go wrong.

What will be will be, it's said, and just a few minutes later I found myself asking how on earth I could have felt anything but fondness and affection for this wonderful course called Leopardstown. The reason for my sudden change of heart? The sheer thrill of seeing Danoli turn in a spectacular performance to spreadeagle the opposition and, at the same time, give his Sun Alliance prospects a timely boost.

This was a victory to savour because Danoli, apparently none the worse for his fall before the race, had been forced to do things the hard way – from the front. The last thing we'd wanted was for him to get bogged down in a muddling pace. So down at the start, Charlie had asked who would make it. There were no takers and he decided to do the donkey work himself. He had the rest of the field in trouble before the final turn and promptly put the issue beyond doubt by asking Danoli to quicken. The response was immediate and electric and he cruised home by ten lengths from Coq Hardi Affair, with What A Question third and Idiot's Venture fourth – all of them top-class horses.

The ease of the victory left no one in any doubt that Danoli was as near a Cheltenham certainty as you could get. Charlie himself was in no doubt. He told me afterwards: 'This is the best prospect I've ever had going to the Festival.'

The only problem we faced was in deciding between the Citroën Supreme Novices Hurdle over two miles and the Sun Alliance Hurdle over two miles and five. In the end we went for the Sun Alliance because, although Danoli had never raced over the longer trip, I felt sure he'd get it. And Charlie had told us he was certain of riding him in the race, whereas he might have to be aboard Sound Man in the Supreme Novices.

The build-up to Cheltenham was tremendously exciting. I'd been so busy training the horse and planning his races that I was largely unaware of the way in which public feeling for him had been gaining ground. Suddenly, it seemed as if some great crusade had gripped the country and that the whole of Ireland was behind him, willing him to win. It was like election fever, with Danoli getting all the votes. Nobody would hear of defeat – it was completely out of the question. Now everybody wanted to speak to me. The phone never stopped ringing, newspaper lads seemed to be camped all around and TV and radio were desperate for interviews. You can imagine what kind of pressure that put me under, a country lad with no great education to speak of and green as grass when it came to handling the media. It's a wonder I came through it all.

The race stands out in my memory as one of the greatest events of my life. I'll never forget it – and neither will I forget the journey over.

5

Cheltenham Goes Hoarse Over Danoli

THE plane started swaying like a kite. I wasn't scared, but perhaps I should have been. I'd never set foot out of the country before, let alone flown in a jet. It was so cramped in there, what with the horses and all, you could hardly swing a cat, even if you'd wanted to. I didn't because I was actually as sick as a dog.

All the boys began worrying about me. They thought it was first-flight nerves, but it was nothing of the sort. They weren't to know that, though. They couldn't possibly have known unless they'd been to a fairground with me when the children were small. Then they'd have understood, right well.

Forget those hundred-mile-an-hour rides that teenagers love; forget things like the Big Dipper and those crazy chairs on rails which whip you round so fast that you leave your stomach behind. You'd need a death wish to go on some of those. I'm talking about slow, easy rides such as the Big Wheel and swing boats and the like. I couldn't even sit on those without my stomach churning. About the only ride I'd have been safe to go on was the kiddies' merry-go-round. Even then I wouldn't have trusted myself.

So when the plane started rocking that little piece, I knew I had no chance whatsoever. I got as sick as could be. Danoli, on the other hand, took the flight well; he must have looked across at me sitting with my head between my knees and thought, 'What an eejit of a trainer I've got.'

In the wind-up, when we landed and all, I could hear a few of the lads saying, 'That's the worst flight ever I was on.' They'd been as nervous as could be themselves but passed it off because they were worried for me.

Yet I'd rather get sick like that in a plane than be seasick any time. At least it was only for 45 minutes. You take to the sea for four or five hours and in the end you feel like lepping off the boat. I went out a couple of different times on an old boat fishing and got as sick as could be.

We were out three or four miles and yer man said, 'Pull in your rods – I'm going out further.'

And I said, 'If you do, let me off. I'm walking back.' I was that bad, I didn't care if she sank. It's a fierce sickness. The funny thing is that the minute she'd come back in and dock and I'd walk out on the yoke, I'd be right again. There'd be no problem with me at all.

Flying now doesn't worry me in that line. Don't get me wrong – I don't like it. I'd rather have my feet on the ground any time. But to think about flying over for Cheltenham – that doesn't cost me at all. Yet if I was going by boat, I'd be sick at the present time just at the thought of it. I definitely wouldn't be looking forward to going. Cheltenham would be the one meeting I'd be trying to avoid.

The three-day Festival started on the Tuesday and Danoli's race, the Sun Alliance, was to open the show on the Wednesday.

There was an atmosphere about the place which I loved; it was Irish wall-to-wall, full of spirit and cheer. I was surprised to see so many women and priests caught up like everybody else in all the hustle and the bustle. It made me realise that this was not so much a race meeting as a wonderful social occasion where the Irish at home and abroad gather once a year for the craic and, hopefully, some winners. In a few cases, big winners.

I devoutly hoped the clergy would be backing Danoli, because you'd imagine they'd be putting down the 'smart money'. They'd know something the rest of us didn't. No need to raid the Poor Box when they got home.

Yet you couldn't mistake a distinctly un-Irish air of gloom hanging over the course after the first day's racing, as if the Festival had still to come to life. Not a winner in sight. Instead of Green Tuesday it had been Black Tuesday. Some well-fancied horses had been turned over, and it knocked our confidence a bit. I got to wondering whether the Irish horses that year weren't as good as the English horses, and if we'd all been getting too carried away about Danoli's chances.

With the arrival of a crisp new day, our hopes rose. With Danoli about to go for Ireland, a mood of optimism grew as the morning wore on. I had the feeling, even the conviction, that the balance would be redressed. With a vengeance.

Come early afternoon, with the crowd pouring through the turnstiles, there was a feeling that deliverance was at hand: this would be the Day of the Irish. Danoli, who was fit to burst, caught the scent of it, too. His physical condition convinced me it would take something special to lower his colours. He was almost kicking down the box in his readiness to get out on the course and fly.

I'd prepared him mentally as well as physically. I'd made sure he was up for it in my pre-race chat with him that morning, when we'd stayed together and prayed together. As far as I was concerned, this wasn't the Sun Alliance, it was the Holy Alliance and Cheltenham would be rocked to its foundations. I'd read him out a few bits from *The Sporting Life* and *The Racing Post* and he'd copped on. He'd received his instructions and knew precisely what to do: lay up with the pace and take the lead when he felt like it, although not too soon. He'd give Charlie Swan the office – let him know when to make his move. He was primed for action and ready to run the race of his life.

As I gave Charlie the leg up on Danoli, I could see that the responsibility of steering the horse to victory rested lightly with him. He was up for it, too. He knew better than anyone how to ride him and there was no need to complicate the issue with last-minute instructions. I'd told the horse what to do; no need to tell the jockey as well. Charlie's face was lit up with that wonderful half-smile he always seems to be wearing and which says everything about a man who's in his right place in the world and absolutely loves the job he's doing. It was as if, to him, the outcome of the race was a foregone conclusion. I could only hope that was the case, because the atmosphere was beginning to get to me. The buzz going round the ground as the horses went down to the start made me shiver with the excitement of it all.

My job was done. It was now up to Charlie and Danoli to bring it on home for Danny O'Neill, who, like myself, was experiencing his first taste of the big-time. If we'd thought we'd 'arrived' with Danoli's participation in the Irish Champion Hurdle, then this made us appreciate that nothing in the National Hunt calendar compares with the magic of Cheltenham.

THERE was big activity in the betting ring, for those brave Irish lads who'd been all but wiped out on the first day were a fiercely determined breed. It would be do or die – Danoli or nothing. They'd be going home rich or they'd be going home with the backsides hanging out of their trousers: there'd be no middle course. So they strapped on their boots, girded their loins and waded into the bookmakers with a ferocity that would have made the Battle of Clontarf in 1014, when King Brian Boru and his men chucked the Danes back into the sea, look like a mere skirmish.

They laid siege to the bookies, smashing into them with rare venom and sustaining the onslaught until the enemy cried out for mercy. 'Enough, enough already!' was heard more than once as the whole line of layers was trapped like boxers on the ropes, with no referee to step in and save them. They received a merciless pounding as one heavyweight wager after another hit home with all the force of a Jack Doyle haymaker. Some notable bets were struck, chief among them a mighty £130,000 to £80,000. Only one name springs to mind with wagers of that magnitude, but whether it was indeed the fearless and legendary J P McManus isn't known and J P isn't saying. But I'm convinced he was the mystery figure and that he wiped out his huge first-day deficit incurred on Gimme Five, which he owned, and Sound Man, in which he had a share, with this bet alone. Of one thing you can be sure: it wasn't T Foley Esq of Aughabeg, Co Carlow. Scores of other hefty bets were recorded, including, at 2-1: £40,000-£20,000, £10,000-£5,000 twice; £8,000-£4,000; £5,000-£2,500; £4,000-£2,000 four times; £2,800-£1,400; £2,000-£1,000 seven times . . . and so it went on as the price was driven down to 15-8 and 7-4: £7,500-£4,000 twice; £3,750-£2,000 twice; £3,500-£2,000. There were numerous other four-figure bets and dozens more of between £500 and £1,000.

Only when the race finally went off a minute late at 2.16 did those bruised and battered bookies get some much-needed respite. Still reeling from the punishment they had taken, the only way open to them was to cling to the hope that some great miracle might occur such as has never before been visited upon the sacred plains of Cheltenham and which would enable them to stave off the imminent threat of insolvency, even bankruptcy. But all the miraculous medals were in the keeping of the Irish and they were fingering them fervently as the horses disappeared round the far side of the course.

The silence was eerie and the portents chilling as the layers stood po-faced on their pitches, looking for all the world like condemned men on the gallows just before the trap door is sprung. Mercifully they did not have long to wait, for a slow, lingering death should never be wished on any of God's children, not even a bevy of bookmakers. The huge roar that engulfed them as Danoli took the lead four out and crested the rise of the hill like an eagle soaring majestically into the sky told them of their fate more readily than words could. The executioner was on his way!

It was an awe-inspiring sight. Danoli's 22 rivals were toiling in his wake and victory seemed a formality. He was running and jumping superbly and, coming to the last, it was a matter not just of whether he'd win but by how far. But in the heat of battle, and with the noise of the crowd at its most deafening, he momentarily took his eye off the hurdle and flattened it, at one and the same time pumping fresh oxygen into a lifeless corps of bookmakers and giving his legion of supporters the feeling that they were about to breathe their last.

They worried unduly, for this was no big deal to Danoli. Having almost thrown the race away, he merely shrugged aside the mishap as if it hadn't occurred and quickened away well. The incident enabled him to have some company during the long run-in, injecting fresh drama into the race. With Dorans Pride coming to grief at the last, it was left to the 10-1 shot Corrouge, with Carl Llewellyn up, to engage him in a pulsating battle to the line. But there was only going to be one winner, for no horse could live with Danoli up that punishing Cheltenham hill. He got home convincingly in the end, by two lengths, to record Ireland's first success in the race since Mister Donovan back in 1982.

The scenes when the horse was led into the winner's enclosure will take some beating, even if the race is run for another hundred years. Charlie Swan had sparked it all when he punched the air with delight as he and Danoli flashed past the post. He was in effect saying to the huge crowd massed up in the stands: 'We've done it, boys. Go and collect your money.' It was the signal for thousands of Irishmen, their wagers won, to charge round the back of the grandstand to the paddock.

And what a victory party they provided. It was the eve of St Patrick's Day and the knees-up started early. It looked and sounded as if the whole of Ireland was there celebrating. Anybody with even a trace of Irish in their blood must have backed the horse and, judging by the scale of the festivities, they'd all had plenty on.

I WAS lifted bodily into the winner's enclosure and, once there, hoisted high on to the shoulders of my enthusiastic compatriots. The same happened to Danny O'Neill. It was one of the biggest, most spontaneous outbreaks of mass hysteria I've ever seen – bigger even than for the great Dawn Run when she won the Gold Cup in 1986. The cheers rang out so loud and so long, I thought they'd never stop. And all of it directed at two men and a horse from the back of beyond in County Carlow. I'll never forget those fabulous, frantic scenes as long as I live.

Nobody can say I was over-dressed for the occasion. There I was in the winner's enclosure in my old pullover, with no jacket; but for the first time in ages I was wearing a tie. It was all so new to me then, being propelled on to the world stage and facing all those Press and television interviews and the like. But there was a bigger ordeal ahead.

It was the biggest shock of my life when the Queen Mother asked me up to her private box. Having finally been let down off the shoulders of those whooping Danoli fans, a steward or envoy or whatever name you'd call him came up and tapped me on the shoulder: 'Excuse me Mr Foley, sir, but the Queen Mother would like to meet you – for just a couple of minutes.' I hadn't a clue what I'd say to her, but the man said she was very nice and so off we went. Now, the Queen Mother is a very gracious and charming lady and we got on so well that two minutes soon turned to ten. But for the life of me I can't remember a word she said, or what I said in return. I was in such a whirl that the memory of it all is just a blur.

I'm learning all the time as regards interviews and such, but I know I'll never change as a person. No matter how big I get in racing, I'll always try to be true to myself. It's the way I was brought up and it's good enough for me. I'd never pretend to be someone I'm not and I'm sure that people would soon see through it. There was no way I was going to put on any airs or graces, even for the Queen Mother, and I'm sure she wouldn't have expected me to. Meeting her was one of the highlights of my life and I remember wondering what they'd make of it all back in Bagenalstown.

As I'd anticipated, it turned out to be a great day all round for the Irish – and particularly Charlie Swan. He went on to take the Coral Cup on Time For A Run and the Festival bumper on Mucklemeg, both trained by Edward O'Grady.

The reception when we got home was heart-warming. People rushed from their houses, cars tooted their horns and half of Carlow flocked to the yard to get a glimpse of Danoli. It was all very emotional. A cousin of mine, Pat Nolan, who's a butcher, came in with tears streaming down his face, threw his arms round Goretti, got back in his car and drove away. He never spoke a word.

If I'd been a drinking man, I'd have been out of my head for days. I know that the celebrations at my brother John's pub at Milltown, and in all the pubs in the vicinity of Bagenalstown, lasted practically until we returned to England three weeks later. This time the venue was Liverpool and the race the Martell Aintree Hurdle, worth more than £30,000 to the winner. Not only was it Grand National Day but the Martell was actually the curtain-raiser to the National, which meant that a huge international television audience would be tuned in. I was delighted because the more people who saw Danoli in action, the happier I'd be. He was a legend in waiting. It was just a matter of time.

With the National the big showpiece race of the day – it was won by comedian Freddie Starr's Miinnehoma – we could relax and enjoy the atmosphere. We felt under no pressure, because Danoli had proved in the Sun Alliance what an exceptional horse he was. There were plenty of Irish at Aintree, of course, but they don't take over the place like they do Cheltenham and the betting on the Martell didn't compare with the Sun Alliance. In fact, I couldn't believe the price of Danoli. For the bookies to put him in at 5-1 after Cheltenham was little more than an insult. At the same time, it presented a great betting opportunity. He was only third favourite behind Flakey Dove and Fortune And Fame and I knew I had him in tip-top shape. He'd come on in leaps and bounds since going down to Fortune And Fame at Leopardstown and was still improving. There was no way in the world I could see him being beaten.

Against all my normal inclinations, I backed him. At that price, I just couldn't restrain myself. And with my confidence at such a pitch, how much do you think I had on? A monkey? Or even five-and-a-half monkeys, as Paddy Bennett had staked on Rua Batric? The truth is I rang home and asked Goretti to put on £50 with a bookie. To me, that's a sizeable bet. Danoli had to be a cast-iron, nailed-on certainty for me to risk even that much. In case you're wondering, it's not that I'm a tight wad – just that I'm not a betting man, except in circumstances like this that are too good to resist.

Looking Ahead: Danoli takes a good look at the first. *(Healy)*

Touchdown: Danoli shows his class. *(Healy)*

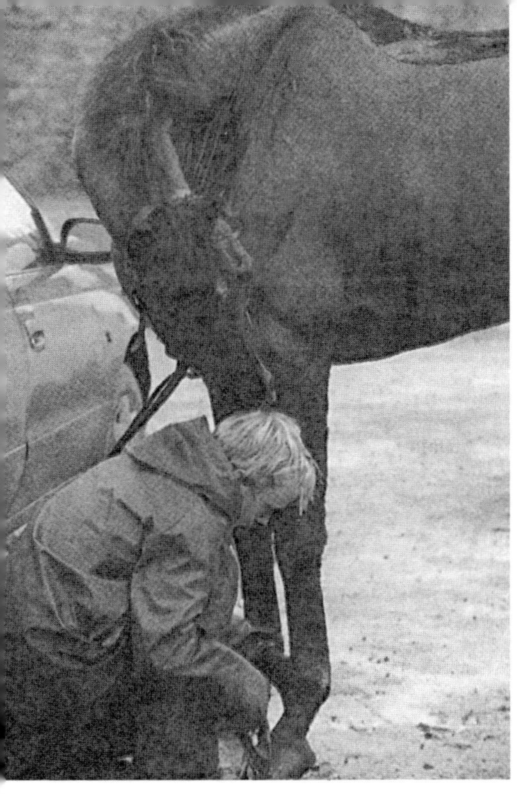

Hay there! Danoli makes a meal of Padraig English's hair. *(Racing Post)*

Easy does it: Danoli on the gallops. *(Racing Post)*

Naas one, Tommy: Danny O'Neill congratulates Tommy Treacy after Danoli's victory in the Quinns of Naas Novices Chase. *(Healy)*

Conquering Hero: Cheltenham goes crazy as Danoli is led in by Danny O'Neill after storming to victory in the Sun Alliance. (*Gerry Cranham*)

Pulling Power: Playful Danoli celebrating his win after the Sun Alliance at Cheltenham with Tom and Sharon Foley, right. *(Star)*

Braveheart: Danoli strides on with shattered leg to win the Martell Hurdle at Aintree. *(Healy)*

Model Patient: Danoli with vet Chris Riggs and Yvonne Rice. *(Mercury Press)*. *Inset*: How Danoli's shattered leg was put back together. *(Mercury Press)*

Holy Orders: Father Dowling blesses Danoli, watched by Noel Hamilton, Tom and Goretti Foley. *(Sporting Life)*

Premier League: Tom Foley with former Taoiseach John Bruton and their children Pat and Emily. *(Healy)*

Poor Goretti. She wasn't used to this kind of thing; but, nevertheless, she did as I said and took the 5-1 available. Danoli opened on the course at 4-1 and drifted to 9-2, his eventual starting price. So by taking 5-1, we'd pinched a shade of odds; it meant that if, as expected, the horse went and won, we'd collect £300 (including our stake) instead of £275. The difference of £25 isn't a fortune, I admit, but it's nice to beat the odds.* As the race unfolded, however, I realised I could have had the five-and-a-half monkeys on Danoli and not had a worry in the world, for he turned it into little more than a procession.

Charlie Swan let him stride out after overhauling the pace-making Muse at the third last and he ran on in brilliant style to win by eight lengths from the veteran Mole Board. In third place, just a neck away, was Fortune And Fame, but it was a distant 20 lengths back to Muse and a farther five to champion hurdler Flakey Dove. It was a bloodless victory and the rapid rate of Danoli's progress in recent months could be gauged by the fact that he'd turned the tables on Fortune And Fame to the tune of almost ten lengths.

Whilst nothing in the world could possibly match the wild and wonderful celebrations that followed Danoli's victory in the Sun Alliance, the cheers that rang out over Aintree, and the reception in the unsaddling enclosure, proved just how much the public had taken the horse to its heart. They'd all been witness to his tenacity and strength in the Sun Alliance; now, in contrast, they'd been treated to an exhibition of supreme authority in the Martell.

There is another side to it. In the Sun Alliance, Danoli looked for all the world as if he was battling courageously to subdue an

*My brother Pat was a good bit braver than me. He had £1,000 on at 5–1. His wife, Anne, celebrated the victory – though not the gambling coup – with 'Tribute to Danoli', which was recorded in a Dublin studio. Local recording artist Richie Kavanagh has also written a song, 'Danoli'. It forms part of a new four-track single to promote his video 'Richie Rides Again', featuring Danoli and myself and Danny and Olivia O'Neill.

opponent at the business end of the race, refusing at all costs to concede defeat. On reflection, that might have been misleading. Without detracting from the ability of the other horses in the race, particularly Corrouge, Danoli gave the impression of running well within himself and merely toying with his rival – letting him play catch-up and then pulling away again like a souped-up sports car. It makes for an exciting race and Danoli does pose that touch of arrogance. It's the mark of all true champions. They can't help taking themselves to the limit to prove their greatness. Sometimes they overdo it but it's something that can't be legislated for in training. I'll just have to warn him he's getting too big for his boots.

I WAS happy and satisfied; more than that, I was ecstatic. After all our early struggles and setbacks, we'd finally produced a horse good enough to win at Cheltenham and Aintree. It was a fantastic feeling to have a star in the stable, and he wasn't back long before we let him away for his summer break on Danny O'Neill's farm. I'd resisted the temptation of running him at Punchestown, where Fortune And Fame was headed. He'd done enough for the season and had earned a holiday. So had I, but I wouldn't be having one. In fact I've never taken a holiday because I wouldn't know what to do with myself. And there are always things to be attended to here in the yard.

As for Danny, he could relax and enjoy the company of Danoli for a few months, along with counting his £30,000 prize-money. Mind you, he'd probably only just finished totting up his near-£40,000 winnings from the Sun Alliance. He was doubtless looking on it all as a nice little sideline to his bone-setting and his work on the farm, and reflecting how wise he'd been not to have sold the horse when he'd had the chance.

These decisions often aren't easy and the only way I know of dealing with them is to ignore what's in your head and listen to your heart – that's where you'll find the answer. And then be man enough to stand by your decision. Danny listened to his heart and he was rewarded many times over, both in terms of money earned and more enjoyment than he could ever have thought possible. Okay, so wife Tess and the girls might have been nagging away at him for new dresses or hats and the like as he sat there in his kitchen gazing fondly at the recent entries in his bank deposit book. Life's full of problems. But I'm sure he could live with that.

Me? I'd been struggling to make ends meet. As Danoli's trainer I received ten per cent of his prize-money; it didn't make me rich but it did help things along a bit. It had been tough getting him to the top, but all the hard work had been worthwhile and after just ten races (eight wins, a second and a third) he was, at the age of six, the finest hurdler in the British Isles bar none. The feeling of fulfilment was immense and now, with the season over, we could take things easier for a month or two.

At the time I had only 15 horses in training and that's all I had room for, as I was still combining training with cattle farming. But with Danoli now famous, people began beating a path to our door. Not literally, of course, because they'd never have found us, but via the telephone. It suddenly started ringing and it rarely stopped. We were flooded with calls from people wanting us to handle their horses.

Success brings its rewards but you have to be ready. I realised that I needed to expand, and quickly. For a start, I'd have to knock down some of the old outbuildings and erect a couple of stable blocks. If all went to plan, it would leave me free to go into training full-time. In the meantime, though, I'd have to lease some boxes to house the new intake.

So I put on my jeans and sneakers and moseyed on down to see music man Denny Cordell.

6

With a Little Help from My Friend

HIS double-barrelled surname never gave Denny Cordell-Lavarack a significant advantage in life. But his music did. Known in these parts as plain Denny Cordell, he was responsible for some of the seminal rock sounds of the sixties and seventies.

His legend lives on in his music and in a horse whose name was inspired by one of his records. He's part of the folklore of this corner of Ireland where horses can make fools of wise men and wise men can make fools of themselves.

Denny was neither wise man nor fool, but he had a touch of genius. He was a free spirit who did what his instincts dictated and never stopped to count the cost.

Having made a fortune in the record business, he came to Ireland to train greyhounds and horses. The fact he knew little about either did not deter him. That was the measure of the man: do what comes naturally and let the music take you.

It was a philosophy that had brought him huge rewards. Born in Buenos Aires and educated in England, he left school at 17 and went to Paris, where he tracked down the jazz trumpeter

Chet Baker and, briefly, became his manager. On returning to London, he took an office job with the Moody Blues management company. They'd been desperately seeking a hit for the band, but without success. It was Denny's big chance. He'd been knocked out by the Bessie Banks song 'Go Now' and persuaded the Moodies to record it. The rest, as they say, is history.

The song became a monster and Denny made £36,000 – not a fortune as fortunes go, but a sizeable chunk of money in the mid-sixties, when £3,000 would have bought an average semi in England and Cliff Richard purchased what was described as a mansion for £20,000. Had Denny decided to come to Ireland then, and not in the late seventies, that £36,000 would have bought him half of Carlow.

But he was only getting started in the music business. He produced the all-time classic 'A Whiter Shade of Pale' for Procul Harum in 1967 and, the following year, a hit version of the Lennon/McCartney number 'With a Little Help From My Friends' for Joe Cocker. He launched Joe in the United States with the legendary 'Mad Dogs and Englishmen' tour, building around him the amazing Grease Band comprising Gary Busey on drums, J J Cale on guitar, Leon Russell on keyboards and Rita Coolidge on back-up vocals. They toured coast-to-coast in a convoy of stretch limos and finished up with a famous appearance at the Woodstock Festival. He also worked with artists like Georgie Fame and The Move.

When he set up an independent label, Shelter Records, he based it in Tulsa but with offices and studios 24 hours from there, in Hollywood. He signed Russell, J J Cale and Phoebe Snow and later turned a band called Mud Crutch into Tom Petty and The Heartbreakers. A few hits later Tom and Denny fell out, a costly court battle followed and Shelter closed down.

Some time previously, around the early seventies, he'd

founded Mango Records with his friend Chris Blackwell, head of Island Records. The story goes that he went to Jamaica, moved into a beach shack and drove to work in a black Ferrari (number plate RAAAS). But Denny wasn't as crazy as he seemed. He landed two big fish in Bob Marley and The Wailers and Toots and The Maytals.

In the late seventies he and Ian 'Flipper' Ross, a founder of Radio Caroline, opened Flippers, a successful roller disco club in Los Angeles. While on America's west coast, he bred and trained greyhounds. But Malibu Beach, where he'd rented a house, clearly wasn't the place to exercise them. It didn't endear him to his film star neighbours and he decided to head back across the Atlantic, this time to Ireland.

The year was 1979 and the property he bought was Corries, just down the road from Aughabeg. With a touch of sentiment, he repainted it in the blue and white of his native Argentina. The training facilities included a half-mile all-weather gallop, starting stalls, 30 acres of paddock and 24 boxes. He read every book he could find on the subject of training and, aided by Bagenalstown handler, Brendan Murphy, bred dogs which raced under the Malibu banner. Yet he won the Waterloo Purse – the Waterloo Cup consolation event – with the unlikely-sounding Some Skunk.

He was soon up and running with the horses. Jim Treacy, formerly head lad to Paddy Mullins, was his right-hand man and Niall McCullagh his stable apprentice. Tommy Treacy would also become apprenticed to him in due course.

Denny had a fairytale start, considering he'd never set foot in a racing yard before coming to Ireland. By his second season, eight of his ten runners had won. He bred and trained Baba Karam, the highest-rated Irish two-year-old colt of 1986, and several other useful performers. They included Modest, who rattled up a sequence of four wins on the trot, the last of them being a Listed win at the Curragh. He also enjoyed success as a breeder at his Kellistown Stud, producing some decent horses in Gorinski, earner of almost £100,000 for Jack Berry, Rebinski, winner of £80,000 in Italy, and Hajade.

I GOT to know Denny quite well over the years and was an occasional visitor to Corries House – though not, I stress, at the wild rock 'n' roll parties that frequently took place there and which were so loud and riotous they could have woken the dead (and in some cases probably did).

With Denny's permission, I'd been taking Danoli down to his all-weather gallop. By the time Danoli became a star, however, his training operation was virtually at an end. We came to an agreement that I'd lease 15 boxes until my new stables were installed, but little did I or anybody else realise – least of all Denny himself – that he had just nine months to live.

I don't know quite why it all went wrong for him. Maybe the tranquil country life and the training of racehorses had been just a rich man's toy, but he grew to love the sport and never tired of it. It's suggested he lost a vast fortune running into eight figures, but I dispute this. You couldn't possibly lose around £10 million running a relatively small 20-horse training operation. If so I, and plenty like me, had better watch out. The true figure was £1 million and it was a loss he could have stood but for having two ex-wives and an extended family to support.

Whatever the way of it, he'd gone back into the music business [as A & R man for Island Records] and, wouldn't you know it, struck gold again with the Limerick band The Cranberries. They'd been discovered by his eldest son, Barney, in Cork in 1993 and became one of the biggest-selling acts in the United States.

Denny died in February 1995 in a Dublin hospital following a short illness. He was 51. His body was taken from Corries by horse-drawn carriage to the Lorum Church of Ireland in Bagenalstown. En route it stopped at his all-weather gallop – a scene so familiar to Danoli and myself. It was an especially sad moment.

The church was packed solid. The mourners at his funeral read like a *Who's Who* of the rock world and included Bono of U2, Paul McGuinness, manager of the mega rock group from Dublin, Chris Blackwell and sixties singer Marianne Faithfull, on whose new album, *A Secret Life*, he had been working. Film actor John Hurt was also present and commentators Ted Walsh and Robert Hall represented horse-racing. I was one of the pall-bearers, along with Jim Treacy.

The congregation sang 'Crimond' and 'O Danny Boy' and the service ended with 'When The Saints Go Marching In'. Denny, I fancy, would have loved the irony in that. His racing silks of red, green and gold – the Rasta colours and those of the County Carlow GAA – were sitting on top of his coffin as he was laid to rest in a corner of the adjacent cemetery. It was only right that he should have been buried in Ireland, where he'd lived for 16 years. I miss his colourful presence at the various race-meetings, particularly Gowran Park, where he was such a popular figure.

Fittingly, a race in his honour is staged there in September each year. It's the Denny Cordell-Lavarack Memorial Fillies Stakes, but it's a Flat race over a mile and a furlong and that rules out my horses. I did the next best thing this year by running, on the same day, the horse I mentioned earlier and whose name you'll all recognise.

It's a seven-year-old by Niniski out of a French mare, Aiguiere, and it was bred by Denny himself. It's owned by Barney Cordell and it's called Go Now, considered by many to be the best song ever recorded by the Moody Blues.

I'm delighted to be training this big bay gelding and, at the same time, helping to perpetuate Denny's legend. I know

Barney has turned down two separate six-figure offers for the horse from a couple of very famous racing ladies, one an owner and one a trainer. He did so because he's dreaming of Grand National glory with Go Now. And why not? Racing is all about hopes and dreams – and they sometimes come true.

Just ask Danny O'Neill.

7

The Call That Broke My Heart

SADNESS, they say, is good for us at times because it opens a window to the soul. If that's the case, mine could do with a bit of double glazing.

Not because of Denny's death particularly, because I wasn't what you'd call a close friend: I was more an acquaintance. But you still feel it when a person goes, especially somebody of the stature of Denny, who had achieved so much. If nothing else, it reminds you of your own mortality.

It's worse with a relative, of course. My father's death in 1980 had been hard to bear and my mother's equally so in 1995. Yet with parents there's a certain inevitability about it all. It doesn't cushion the blow or make the loss any the less painful. But at least it doesn't come as a total shock.

The worst kind of deaths are those involving the young, because they're snatched away before they've really had a chance to live. It always seems such a waste. And when that death is sudden and unexpected, it can cut you in two. It's why I'll never forget the first day of June, 1994.

Danoli's successes at Cheltenham and Aintree had given us all such a lift. The close season was upon us. The new horses had started to arrive. We could give ourselves a small pat on the back for a job well done and be excused for thinking that all was right with the world. Then something happens to shake you up like nothing else on earth and serve as a warning that the life we all treasure so dearly and believe will never end can be snuffed out in the blink of an eye.

I'd had plenty of banter over the years with my niece, Breda, the daughter of my brother Ger. As a youngster, she'd often skip down the lane that separates our house and training quarters from Ger's bungalow that sits out facing the road like a white-painted doll's house. And in later years, when she'd blossomed into a young woman, we'd enjoy the craic during my journeys backwards and forwards with the horses. Tall, dark haired, blue-eyed and still only 19, she had brightened many a day with her vitality and humour. She was as thrilled and excited as the rest of the family about the exploits of Danoli, and she adored him.

On that fateful morning, the phone had rung early, just after 6.30, and given us quite a start. As I lifted the receiver, it flashed through my mind that perhaps it was an owner holidaying abroad who'd had a few and forgotten the time difference. But I instantly recognised the voice of my brother, Jim, coming clear across the trans-Atlantic airwaves from 3,500 miles away in Toronto.

As soon as he spoke, I realised something was wrong. There was no cheery greeting and no small talk, as you'd normally expect. Instead, the message he brought was like a kick in the stomach from one of the horses: 'I've some bad news. Breda has been killed in a car crash in San Francisco.' The walk of a hundred or so yards to the top of the lane felt like a mile. My heart was heavy and my step laboured. It was as if the world was closing in on me. The rest is just a blur of memory: the sorrow and pain as I spoke the words that I realised would tear Ger, his wife Breda and their son Ger Jnr, then 16, apart; the look of shock and disbelief on their faces as the horror of it all sunk in; the helplessness you feel when attempting to console a family consumed with grief over the loss of a loved one. Never, as long as I live, will I forget that scene of utter anguish and despair.

The details of the death which emerged later made young Breda's passing no easier to bear. She and two second cousins, the O'Sullivan sisters, Rose and Irene, from Ennis in County Clare, had been on their way to a Bryan Adams concert. A friend's car in which they were travelling spun out of control and overturned. The three girls had been in the back. Breda and Rose were catapulted through a window and killed instantly. Irene survived.

Breda had been gaining work experience in the States, caring for the young and elderly. Her gentle nature fitted her perfectly for both roles. Ironically, she'd been due back in Ireland in three weeks. But instead of returning home cock-a-hoop with tales of her great adventure in a land of opportunity for every Irish man and woman, her broken body was flown home for burial.

The bill was £17,000 but Ger didn't have to foot a penny. Friends and relatives rallied round and £21,000 was raised within just a few days. He donated the remaining £4,000 to BEAM, a support group for the mentally handicapped in the Barrow Valley area.

They say it was the biggest funeral seen in Bagenalstown. The queue of mourners stretched for more than a mile from the gates of the cemetery. Silent and solemn they stood, in tribute to one of their own. It's deeply touching how death unites a town and its people: a collective coming together, a closing of ranks against the outside world, an expression of grief shared.

Ger and his family are still coming to terms with their loss. I know they'll cope. Breda left them – and me – with wonderful memories.

8

The Challenge That I Could Not Ignore

LIFE went on. By October, our new horses were finding their feet and the jump season was back in full swing. I was busier than ever operating between Aughabeg and Corries, but I had no complaints – it's how I preferred it.

Danoli was back in the fold but, boy, did he need some work. He'd been spoilt over at Danny O'Neill's during the summer and I can't say I was surprised. After all, what are you to do when you own a horse who's made headline news and swelled your bank balance by £70k in a matter of weeks? When all your sons and daughters want to make a fuss of him and show him off to their friends? When people calling in to see him insist on stuffing him full of sugar lumps and mints and heaven knows what?

We managed to get him into some short of shape by November and his campaign for the season kicked off in the Morgiana Hurdle, a Grade Two event over two-and-a-quarter miles at

Punchestown. This, you'll remember, was the race we skipped the previous year in favour of the Ballycaghan Hurdle.

The plan for the term was a crack at three big races: the AIG (Europe)-sponsored Irish Champion Hurdle at Leopardstown in January, the Smurfit Champion Hurdle at Cheltenham in March and a defence in April of the Martell Aintree Hurdle. After that, the only certainty was that he'd go off again to Myshall for the summer and come back to us carrying more tonnage than Danny himself.

Maybe then we'd send him chasing, which had always been in the back of my mind. If he could jump the big ones he'd be a Gold Cup horse, no doubt about it, because he had the class. Charlie Swan had been banging on about it since the Sun Alliance. He said if we went back to Cheltenham for the Gold Cup, we'd get the same reception all over again. He was right when he talked about the 'same reception' because we couldn't possibly get a bigger one. Ever. Unless they went completely berserk and tore the place down. I wouldn't like to be a steward that day.

But first things first. There's many a slip, as they say, and if there was one thing I'd learned in this game, as well as life in general, it was never to count my chickens.

It came as no surprise that Danoli was virtually unbackable at Punchestown. He was a 1-5 shot and Charlie rode a beautiful race on him. Apart from a blunder at the second last, which he dived at, his jumping was faultless. But I wasn't much worried about Danoli making the occasional mistake because it was a result of his being in front too long. I joked to the Press lads that he takes his eyes off the hurdles because he's trying to look round and see where the others are.

In truth he was a bit rusty but, once Charlie asked him, he strode out impressively. He made all the running and powered home eight lengths clear of Diplomatic, who had Alligator Joe snapping at his heels in third.

The beauty of having a champion like Charlie on board is that he's always switched on, always thinking. Bearing in mind the possibility of Danoli being a future Gold Cup contender, he was anxious to get him jumping like one. In effect, he used the race as a public schooling session to educate him for a chasing career. He kicked Danoli into his hurdles because he wanted him to jump them big, like he'd have to do when he made the switch to the larger obstacles. According to Charlie, if the horse were allowed to 'fiddle' his way over hurdles he'd likely try to do the same over fences – with disastrous results.

Danoli, of course, was blissfully unaware of what we had in mind for him. He was absolutely full of himself in the winner's enclosure, ready for all kinds of mischief. First he butted Charlie and sent him flying. Then he tried to take off with me. It was his way of telling us, 'I'm glad to be back.'

Charlie got it right when he said, 'Riding Danoli is just like driving a Rolls-Royce. If anything had come to me, he'd have slipped into second gear and taken off.' Well, I've never been in a Rolls but obviously that doesn't apply to Charlie; he could afford a fleet of them, the money he earns. Joking aside, he's ridden enough top horses to know if he's on something special. And when I tell you Danoli was only 80 per cent fit after his seven months on the sidelines, and that I was fully prepared for him to lose, you get some idea of the improvement he had in him. It's always a relief to get the season's first race over with, particularly when your horse isn't properly tuned. But things were to hot up sooner than I'd have liked.

Danoli's next outing was a month later in the Hattons Grace Hurdle, a Grade One event at Fairyhouse, the Irish Grand National course in Meath where previously he'd made his debut over timber. The Hattons Grace was an important race with a winner's purse of £25,000. It attracted not only a field of top horses – including Atours, now gaining a big reputation in

England with David Elsworth, and Dorans Pride – but a whole army of reporters from national newspapers in England and Ireland. The huge crowd gave Danoli a Cheltenham-style reception, as Damien McElroy reported in the *Irish Independent*: 'It's a tribute to Danoli's drawing power that an attendance of 8,000 turned up for the televised session, racecards were sold out and the traffic jam on the way to the track was akin to Easter Monday.'

The race itself was something of a grudge match between Danoli and Dorans Pride – or rather between myself and Michael Hourigan. It could have been billed as the Word Championship of Racing.

Usually I'm the most placid, easy-going person you could find; but if I do have a weakness it's that I'm fiercely protective of Danoli. And I'm afraid it got to me when Michael suggested Dorans Pride would have won the Sun Alliance but for falling at the last. My hackles rose. I considered the comment detracted from my horse's performance and I wasn't having any.

Because of it, I felt Danoli's reputation was at stake. I had him wound up more than I'd wanted at this stage of the season, but the Press had been building up the contest and the pressure on me was fierce. To give you an idea of just how fierce, the phone was hot for a week before the race. Like my mother before me, I'd never ducked a challenge and I wasn't going to start now, even though Danoli was carrying top weight of 12 stones and the testing ground was all against him.

In the wind-up, Danoli gave Dorans Pride 5lb and a four-length beating. I felt as if I'd won the Lotto. I couldn't help myself from saying afterwards: 'No horse fell today, so that might keep some lads from talking.' I wanted to let Danoli do the talking and he did just that. I got a lot of pleasure from it.

Racing is a competitive business but, on the whole, relations between the people in it are cordial. You're all striving for the same thing, success, and there's room for everybody. However, when the atmosphere becomes suddenly tense or highly-charged, as sometimes happens, then a long fuse can quickly become a short one and you're bound to get the occasional flashpoint. Especially when you're as passionate about a horse as I am about Danoli. Michael and I did have a few words in the stable area, but we're both grown men and we soon forgot about it. Afterwards I went over to him, shook his hand and said: 'No hard feelings.'

But I didn't feel as charitable towards Dorans Pride's wealthy Mayo-born owner, Tom Doran. I read recently that he fought his way through the huge crowd in the winner's enclosure at Cheltenham and – despite the disappointment of his horse's last-fence fall – sportingly congratulated me on Danoli's victory. Whereupon I'm supposed to have said: 'If your horse had stayed on his feet, we'd still have beaten you.'

The truth is that I never met Tom Doran until the Hattons Grace Hurdle, which was nine months after Cheltenham. I'd been challenged by someone reputedly acting on his behalf to a £20,000 sidestake for this race – just Danoli and Dorans Pride, wherever they finished, regardless of whether either of them won. I didn't take the bait and I heard later that he'd backed down on it. But it made me doubly determined that we'd beat Dorans Pride and after the race I told Tom Doran that I didn't like his way of doing business. I didn't give him much credit.

As to the race itself – or I should say two races – Danoli was superb. The first race was when Pimberley Place set off at such a lick that he was soon 30 lengths in front and racing on his own. The second involved the chasing group, which was being led by Charlie and Danoli. By the third last they'd managed to collar Pimberley Place and were setting sail for home. Dorans Pride and Atours moved up menacingly but Danoli settled the issue with a great jump at the second last. It was as if he'd known just when to produce it to put paid to the chances of the other two. To quote

Michael Clower in *The Sporting Life*, 'Danoli flew the second last and left the challenges of Dorans Pride and Atours floundering in the mud.' I couldn't have put it better myself.

Charlie didn't even get serious with Danoli, who'd been backed down from evens to 4–6. He could hardly contain himself as he held court afterwards, telling the Press: 'This is an amazing horse. He only starts racing when something comes to him and the crowd were making so much noise, I thought something must have been trying to do just that. Pimberley Place went such a gallop and was so far in front that he did us no favours, because Danoli relaxed at the head of the chasing group. It was only when he heard the others coming at us turning for home that he really grabbed hold of his bridle and headed for the line. Full credit to the horse: he quickened every time I asked him and jumped really well when it mattered.'

Britain's now-retired former champion jockey, Peter Scudamore, was equally enthusiastic: 'Danoli's a real racehorse. The other pair were queuing up to have a crack at him two out, but he saw them off with something to spare.'

Richard Dunwoody, who rode the unplaced Magic Feeling, joined in the chorus of praise: 'It was pretty testing ground and Danoli deserved full marks for defying top weight. He showed his ability when he seemed to be vulnerable to the other two after the second last. He's a worthy Champion Hurdle favourite.'

Danny O'Neill could scarcely believe his eyes and his ears. He thought it was Cheltenham all over again and you could understand why. We had to fight our way through to the unsaddling enclosure as throngs of excited racegoers swarmed to catch a glimpse of Danoli. The raucous cheers rang out with such fervour, you'd have thought you were at an eighties Tory Party conference as the Iron Lady swept grandly into the hall. Through it all, Charlie sat astride the horse like a king returning from victorious battle. An ear-splitting smile creased his features and he acknowledged his and the horse's supremacy like a bishop dispensing blessings at an open-air Mass.

Danny had with him a cousin who'd never been to the races before and another relative who'd travelled from London for the occasion. They couldn't believe such scenes. It was as if – in soccer terms – Manchester United had thumped Liverpool in a top-of-the-table clash, or vice versa, and the fans had been allowed to pour on to the pitch to celebrate.

I was uplifted by the whole experience, but my old friend fate has a funny habit of putting you right up there with the angels and then turning round and kicking you in the teeth.

You'd think, from everything Charlie had been saying to the Press, that Danoli was a wonder horse who could never be beaten. It's true – well, at least the first part. He is a wonder horse, but he can still get turned over, the same as any other horse. There are several factors that come into play: the state of the ground, failing to secure a clear run, being bumped, a poor jump or a fall, jockey error and, most unlikely of all in my view, a misjudgement by the trainer! It pains me to have to admit, therefore, that I was responsible for Danoli's defeat in his final race of 1994 – the Bord na Gaeilge Christmas Hurdle run over two miles and six at Leopardstown three days after we'd stuffed the turkey and then ourselves.

Too much Christmas pud? Possibly, but hardly likely to affect my judgement. One too many on Christmas Day? I don't drink. But something definitely muddled my thinking over Christmas and, looking back, I can only conclude that perhaps – in the name of charity – I felt it right to give somebody else a chance. That somebody, as it turned out, being my former sparring partner Michael Hourigan.

Or maybe, it being Leopardstown, the jinx returned to haunt me. Danoli had lost there at the corresponding meeting twelve months earlier. Remember it? When the car broke down and I had to take him out of the box and stick him in a lorry? The ghosts of Christmas past . . . ?

Whatever, I went against all my natural instincts by allowing Danoli to run when I suspected he was unwell. It's not the fact that Dorans Pride got his revenge that eats away at me, though in all conscience that was bad enough. Had the race been run on its merits, I'd have accepted defeat graciously. But Danoli didn't just lose – he was beaten out of sight. He was a 2-1 on shot but ran like a cart-horse. And I'm sure Michael won't accuse me of sour grapes when I say I shouldn't have let him run that day. The horse had coughed once or twice and I should have pulled him out. No question. The reason I didn't was because people would have been bitterly disappointed if he hadn't run, not least the Leopardstown management. Danoli puts thousands on the gate and they'd have been gutted. Others still might have thought we were ducking a rematch with Dorans Pride.

It's fatal to give way to pressure and run your horse when he isn't right. It will never happen again, you can be sure of that. Danoli will always come before any other consideration in that line. It was the first bad race he'd run; and the fact he finished 25 lengths adrift of Dorans Pride will tell you how sick he must have been.

It meant our intended crack at the Irish Champion Hurdle at Leopardstown in the late January of 1995 had to go by the board. Danoli was still coughing and the vets couldn't agree what was wrong. One vet wanted this, another vet wanted to do something else and there was a third vet who didn't want him to run again that year. Then the coughing stopped and Danoli appeared to be all right. Whatever had been wrong with him – a bit of a chest infection, perhaps, or a touch of 'flu – he seemed to have got over it.

Meantime, there was a rake of different stuff being sent to me by a vet from Cork. I got on to Danny and said, 'Look it, I don't agree with what's going on with the horse. The best thing you can do is take him home and let this vet treat him at your place. As far as I'm concerned, he's not coming near Danoli. He's sending me up stuff to give him, but he's never told me what's wrong with the horse and in my opinion there's not a thing wrong with him.'

Danny asked me what I wanted to do. I said I'd like to get in an independent vet – the best in the business – to check out the horse. And that if there was anything wrong with him, I wanted to know it.

So we got a top man from the Curragh, Keiran Bredin, to come down and check Danoli over. He examined him and said, 'Take out the horse tomorrow and work him. There's not a thing wrong with him.'

I was pleased to learn I'd been right, but this was no time for self-praise. We'd lost a lot of unnecessary time and this would affect the build-up to Cheltenham. It meant we'd have to go straight for the Smurfit Champion Hurdle in mid-March without a prep race, which was hardly ideal. But I reckoned I could get him pretty straight without one.

Danoli had been ante-post favourite for the race following the Hattons Grace Hurdle. But the disappointment of the Christmas Hurdle at Leopardstown, and the fact he hadn't raced since, had placed doubts in the minds of the bookies. He ended up 4–1 joint favourite with Large Action, but somebody other than myself and Charlie and Danny must have fancied him because a bet of £20,000–£5,000 was struck. Even so, he carried nowhere near the level of punter confidence that had been behind him for the Sun Alliance the previous year, when the bookies were running for cover. Still, he was laid to take £70,000 from the ring, which proved he hadn't been entirely deserted.

In the event – and with the soft ground not helping him – he ran like a champion. As in the previous year, we'd had our little heart to heart beforehand; he'd learned his lines and but for a terrible mistake at the third last, which he flattened when moving up to challenge for the lead, I reckon he'd have won. That blunder put paid to his chances; he nearly fell and his momentum and stride pattern were lost. Otherwise he might have been able to recover and mount a challenge up the Cheltenham hill. As it was he ran on in his usual courageous way to finish third, beaten five lengths and two by Alderbrook and Large Action. To put this defeat in its proper perspective, take a look at the famous names who finished behind him that day: Fortune And Fame, Mysilv, Absalom's Lady, Atours, Mole Board, Montelado, Jazilah, Destriero, Granville Again, Land Afar and Bold Boss. Some field, that.

Danoli hadn't been out of the first four throughout the race. Charlie said he was travelling really well until he clouted the third last, but afterwards hung badly and was probably a bit sore. Nevertheless, third-place prize money in a race like the Champion Hurdle was still well worth having and Danny could amuse himself by counting out another £18,855 before we'd be back in Liverpool in three weeks for a second crack at the Martell Aintree Hurdle.

I wasn't disappointed at finishing third because I knew full well it was the mistake that had cost Danoli. The interrupted preparation hadn't helped but I remained convinced that he had the beating of any horse in Britain and Ireland – even the brilliant Alderbrook who, before turning to hurdling, had established himself as a class act on the Flat by winning the Group Two Prix Dollar at Longchamp.

However, I didn't begrudge owner, Ernie Pick, and Lambourn trainer, Kim Bailey, their victory and Kim's tears in the winner's enclosure after breaking his Cheltenham duck showed the enormous pressure he must have been under. The emotion of the moment clearly got to him and it proved that big boys do cry. For Kim's a giant, and not only in build. He won the Grand National a few years back with Mr Frisk and you'd think nothing could top that for emotion. It goes to show how much Cheltenham means to people.

With the Martell Hurdle on the horizon, we didn't have time to dwell on Danoli's defeat, which was a good thing. In any case I had no doubts that he'd put the record straight by carrying off the Aintree crown for the second year in succession.

As you know, I was right. Yet the way things turned out, I'd give anything to have been wrong. The spoils of victory sometimes aren't worth the price that has to be paid.

9

He's Coming Home!

THE summer and autumn of '95 should have been among my happiest. However, because of Danoli's terrible injury in the Martell Hurdle, they were seasons of uncertainty and, at times, despair. The victory won him the Cartier National Hunt Award for best hurdling performance – but it didn't ease our pain.

We were missing Danoli so much, it almost hurt. And more worried about him than words can say. Not a day passed without us thinking of him languishing there in the unfamiliar surrounds of Leahurst. He had our prayers and the prayers of countless others to comfort him. He had, too, the devoted care of the staff at Leahurst, who showered him with love and affection. But through it all they were a foster family, doing their best to make him feel wanted; his real family were hundreds of miles away across the Irish Sea, eating their hearts out. We knew he must be missing us as much as we were missing him, which only made it worse. If only horses could talk on the telephone – it would have made it so much easier, for us and for him.

There was a perverse kind of logic to it all. We realised we could have taken him from Leahurst any time we wished and had him treated by a veterinary team at the Curragh. I'm sure Danny O'Neill would have gone along with it if that's what we'd wanted. But we had to be sensible. The horse was in the best possible hands and to have brought him home before he was ready would have been a mistake. More than that, it would have been irresponsible. Danny and I had confidence in Chris Riggs and his team. We had to let them see it through.

Chris would ring from time to time and tell us how it was going. He was always positive and reassuring, but the uncertainty of it all was too much to bear. I decided I'd fly over and see for myself. I went with Ger Foley (a family friend and not my brother of the same name) because Ger knew England and I didn't and he said he'd come with me. Danoli was delighted to see me. He thought I'd come to take him home and felt a mite sorry for himself when he realised that wouldn't be the case; but of course I made a big fuss of him and he knew then that he hadn't been forgotten – or forsaken.

The veterinary team explained everything and showed me all the X-rays. They told me what they'd had to do and pointed out the variety of things that could still go wrong; but they seemed happy enough with his progress. They were that little bit hopeful.

I can't pretend it was easy parting once more from Danoli. But it was nothing like as distressing as before when, straight after his injury, we'd had to leave him in a strange place with unknown faces all around him. Then, he must have thought I was abandoning him. Now, he seemed to have accepted the situation. He'd become used to his surroundings and it was a comfort to know he hadn't been fretting. The best news of all was that he appeared to be on the mend.

Danoli's rehabilitation continued. Another month passed, during which we were in constant contact with Chris Riggs. I decided to go over again and have another look at him. This time he looked happy in himself. Because of his condition, they'd been forced to cut down on his food. He'd lost a lot of weight as a result but, generally, he was in good order. He'd apparently endeared himself in a big way to the staff at Leahurst; everybody there had been keen to look after him and feed him carrots and fruit and the like. I'm convinced that no team of people could have done better for him. I give them full credit in every way. They'd tried to keep him as content as they possibly could.

Eventually, after about two months, Chris Riggs decided Danoli could come home. He said he'd reached the stage where everything he was now doing for the horse could be done by us at Aughabeg. I rang to say we'd be flying in on the Saturday. He asked me where I'd be landing and I told him Cambridge, explaining that I had no idea where that was. As you can appreciate, geography isn't my strong point. I can find my way around Ireland all right, but that's about it. Chris said Cambridge was about 180 miles from Leahurst and he'd have to bring Danoli to us by ambulance. He explained that it wouldn't be fair on the horse to travel that kind of distance – and over to Ireland – all in one day; he might not be up to it. He said that, instead, he'd come down the day before and stay with Danoli overnight.

So he set off with the horse and brought him to Cambridge. He got him stabled at some veterinary college he knew and we were to pick up the horse there at around four o'clock on the Saturday. But we got in early and he was still there with a friend, so he took us out for a meal and came back and waited around with us. The plane that brought us over that day was going to France to pick up some more horses and then returning to take us back to Ireland. When it arrived, Chris collected Danoli from the college and brought him out to the plane. He got him aboard and checked him over to make sure everything was right. He said that if the horse wasn't happy, he'd fly over with us and then fly home again. But there was no need. All seemed well with Danoli and we were able to bring him back ourselves.

His spell at the veterinary hospital cost around £5,000 and I thought it reasonable for two months' keep. I know little about hospitals, thanks be to God, but if I were looked after the same as Danoli was at Leahurst, I'd have no complaints. It was the way they took him to heart and pampered him that really got home. There was no way you could repay the amount of time and effort they'd put into the horse. If ever we win the Gold Cup, Chris Riggs is the man I'd love to have standing there beside it. If anyone deserves to say, 'I'm the one who fixed up this horse to win the Gold Cup', it's him. In fact we owe a great deal to all the people involved, from the ordinary staff at the hospital to the racecourse vets, the ambulance driver and the police. I can't praise them highly enough. It was only through their care and compassion that Danoli was able to survive his ordeal.

Looking back on the race, I'm just grateful we didn't have another flight to jump. If we had, there'd be no Danoli today. We didn't realise at the time how near the horse was to being killed; it was a matter of maybe another half a furlong. There was only half a bone there in the leg and it would have gone in bits. People go on about the qualities of courage and determination in a horse, but Danoli showed the true meaning of those words. He still kept running, still kept going through all the pain – it was that important to him to win. Nobody will ever know how brave he was. You see horses pulling up with only small things wrong with them, yet he was on three legs and no one even knew he was injured.

Somebody's prayers were answered that day. Whose, I don't know. But I'm certain in my heart and soul that somebody somewhere was looking after us. If I knew who it was, I'd go down on my knees and thank them. The horse was so near to being put down that it makes me think we're not half grateful enough to have him back and to see him turn out the way he did. The vast crowd went home from Aintree knowing nothing about it. But masses of people – mainly English – rang next day saying they were out on a golf course or wherever when they heard about Danoli being injured. Many said they cried when they read about it and that the tears fell on to his photograph on the page. Then came the cards – hundreds of them – from all kinds of well-wishers.

It can be a hard old world at times and it does your heart good to know that people can be so kind. Complete strangers you'd never get the chance to meet had taken the time and trouble to sit down and compose their messages of hope and cheer. Naturally, children's cards were the most touching and at the same time the most amusing, because they'd illustrate them with drawings of the horse laid up in hospital. All I can say is that the imagination of a child knows no bounds.

Danoli was surrounded by these cards during his stay at Leahurst. I'm told the staff there read them out to him. I'm sure this great weight of affection got through to him. He'd have understood. It would have made him realise the love and loyalty he'd inspired in people.

If ever a braver or more popular horse has set foot on a racecourse, I haven't heard of him.

10

Tears and Cheers as Danoli Battles Back

IT felt good to be back in Dublin. Danoli was pretty pleased about it, too. In fact he was full of himself as he walked down the ramp from the plane, his leg a mass of bandages, to be greeted by a battery of clicking cameras.

Besides the Press, there were children from a school for the handicapped. Danoli was their hero and they'd heard on TV that he was on his way. Their banner said: 'WELCOME HOME DANOLI.' I was visibly moved. For these little ones with all their problems to have made it to the airport to say their hellos and give Danoli their support showed a real generosity of spirit. If they'd had room on the banner, I'm sure it would have said, 'We hope you're all better now.'

Eventually we were able to load up Danoli and head home with him. About three miles out from Aughabeg we came to a road where we used to walk him each day for exercise. As we got there, he suddenly realised where he was and started to whinny. He whinnied and whinnied like you've never heard before and he never stopped until we got him back home. And he walked out of the box the very same as if there'd never been anything wrong with him. He was thrilled to bits.

Next morning, we went out to saddle up the other horses and I couldn't believe the carry-on of him. He began whinnying and lepping and bucking because he thought one of the saddles was going on him. I had to get Goretti to stay in the 'house' with him that day while we were riding out the other horses. But Danoli's so smart, he knew that he wasn't back to work and he accepted it from then on. No one had to stay with him after that. He just used to stand there and watch the others being led out to work and left it at that.

He stood there for another two or three months. We used to take him out and walk him round a bit but that was it. From time to time we'd get X-rays taken and send them over to Chris Riggs. He'd look at them and tell us everything was going right and that we could do a little bit more with him.

Then it got to the stage where we couldn't manage him at all. He was getting too full of himself, lepping and jumping and cavorting around. So I got in touch with Chris and told him the horse was becoming a handful. We could manage him fine, but I was worried he'd damage the leg. Chris suggested we start swimming him, which was handy enough because my brother John has a few horses and he'd just built an equine pool at his place there in Milltown, close to Garryhill where we all went to school. So it worked out well.

John has a pub and a haulage business as well as his stables, so he's plenty busy. He put in the pool for the horses because the nearest one was at the Curragh, forty miles away. He already had a pool there for public swimming, so it made good sense. Now trainers come from as far afield as Cork to swim their horses.

Anyhow, we got Danoli swimming and I can give you the precise date. Etched into an upright support beam in the pool is the following entry: '2/9/95 – Danoli's first swim here.' I believe it was John's eldest son, Robert, who decided to record this great moment in history.

As it happened, Danoli turned out to be an amazing swimmer. I wasn't too surprised, because it's in his nature, but he's as much a competitor in the water as he is out on the track. If there were swimming races for horses he'd be just as hard to beat. In human terms, he'd be Olympic class.

With swimming, you have the benefit of being able to gallop the horse against the pressure of the water without him having to put a foot to the ground. They say that five minutes in the pool is equivalent to a two-and-a-half mile run – but without the risks associated with putting pressure on the joints. We took him to John's twice a week and he absolutely loved it. After each swim he went into the 'dryer' – a small room containing two six-inch pipes that blast out warm air with such force that it's hard to keep your feet. Danoli loved that, too. He's a real glutton for punishment.

We used to walk him home from the pool and that was grand – for a while. He got so fit from the swimming and the walking that they weren't taking enough out of him and he became full of himself again. It got to the stage where we couldn't walk him home. We got back to Chris Riggs and he advised saddling him and riding him home. So we did that and it worked out grand again. Noel Hamilton used to ride him and I'd drive in front with the car and the box, keeping my eye on things.

Then it got where he wasn't safe to ride on the road. He'd go backwards and sideways and every way in it. We decided then that we couldn't continue because he could fall and hurt himself or do some other kind of damage. You just never knew what might happen.

I got back to Chris Riggs again and he said, 'Right – take him out on the track. Walk him round and gently trot him and see how he goes.'

So we started out on the track with him. We walked and turned him and the like, but he'd get bits of notions and take a piece of a gallop for himself. We decided to say nothing about it to anybody because we knew we'd be in trouble for allowing it to happen. But he was so full of beans that Noel couldn't hold him.

Finally, Chris Riggs said he'd come over and see the horse. I was pleased because then he could assess the situation for himself and we'd get a few things sorted out. He took a good look at Danoli and X-rayed the injured leg. His verdict was that everything was going okay. I explained that we were having nothing but problems with the horse because we were restricted to walking and turning him on the gallop; he'd become too much of a handful and wanted to take off. He said to let him go a small bit, but to be careful not to overdo it. At last we were getting a bit more rope to play around with.

We took him out and started doing pieces of work, but possibly we were doing more than we should have done because we couldn't always hold him. It was frustrating beyond belief and I decided we were going to have to let him back in proper work. There was no way we could stay like this forever, doing just a small piece with him. So I got on to Chris Riggs again.

He said he had a good friend in America, a top man who specialised in this type of injury. He'd showed him some of Danoli's X-rays and said, 'Leave it with me. I'll have a chat with him and we'll see what happens.'

Chris got on to this vet in America. He was weighing up whether it would be better to start back doing a little bit of work with the horse or to leave him for a period and do nothing with him. It was a tricky problem because apparently arthritis could set in if you didn't work the joint and it could set in if you worked it too much. It was a matter of striking the right balance and deciding which way would be best. Danoli had only a certain amount of flexibility in the joint and Chris advised me to keep massaging it. The horse didn't want that at all; he was getting all worked up and it was sore for him, reminding him, and so we started doing a little piece more with him. Each time we did, Danoli responded and eventually he started to work well with us. I told Chris and he was happy with it.

But we had another problem and it was on account of his diet. When we started working him seriously, he wouldn't eat for us. He'd been on only 5lb of feed a day at Leahurst and we were trying to get him up to 15–20lb a day. He'd been on 25lb when he won his big races at Cheltenham and Aintree, so this was a real worry. We just couldn't get him to eat at all. Because of the diet, his stomach had contracted. Even though he was back in work and burning up the calories, it was the devil's own job to get his intake up to anything like it had been before. We kept firing away, but it would take time and patience to get that right.

Autumn came and an incident occurred that could so easily have been fatal for Noel Hamilton:

> 'It was 18 October 1995. Some things you never forget and I'll always have good reason to remember that date. Danoli still wasn't back in full work and I was walking him round the all-weather. Tom said to take him round once more and I did so. But whatever way it happened, Danoli tripped and fell and rolled over on top of me. I heard a crack but didn't know whether it was him or me. I kind of hoped it wasn't him after all he'd been through with the leg.
>
> 'As luck would have it, it was me. My hip was broken. It wouldn't have been so bad if there hadn't been nine fractures. The hip, or what was left of it, was also badly dislocated and it finished me as a race-rider. I'll end up with a false hip eventually, but I count myself lucky. It might have been a whole lot worse. I could easily have been crushed to

death. It's funny how they were able to fix up Danoli and yet they couldn't fix me up. But then I wasn't a patient at Leahurst. Like the advertisement says, I'm not bitter. I've forgiven Danoli and it's great that I'm still able to ride him out each day.'

Around that time we had another good horse, a four-year-old by the name of Moon Man. During all the heartache of Danoli's injury and recuperation, I had it in the back of my mind that if the worst came to the worst and Danoli was unable to race again, Moon Man was ready to take over where he'd left off. I rated the horse that highly. He'd won his two bumpers and ran out in his only race over hurdles, but that wasn't a bother.

It was 4 November and we had him in at Navan. He was up against some good horses, one of which – That's My Man – was after winning a couple of bumpers and a couple of hurdles. Despite the quality of the opposition, Moon Man was about eight lengths clear coming to the second last and cruising to victory when he broke his near foreleg – the same one as Danoli – and had to be destroyed. It was such a tragedy, such a waste. Conor O'Dwyer, who was riding him, told us he only had the horse in second gear. That will tell you how good he was.

It was my 49th birthday and it wasn't a happy one. I was at my lowest ebb, mentally and physically. When you've been battling for months against all the odds to get the star of the stable back to fitness and then the best young prospect in the yard gets killed, it's hard to come to terms with. I was upset, too, for Moon Man's owners, John Dollard and Paul Adams, who'd bred the horse. Theirs was by far the greater loss. The death of promising young horses can only be described as a tragedy. It's a dangerous game we're in, both for the animals themselves and the jockeys. They're the bravest of the brave and we should never for a moment underestimate the risks they take.

In cases like this, you have to try and put the sadness of it all behind you; it's easier said than done because you never quite forget a horse like Moon Man and I've tortured myself with thoughts of how good he might have become. I'm convinced he'd have been one of the jumping greats.

Meanwhile, we struggled on with Danoli. The feeding problem apart, we were gradually succeeding with him and felt reasonably happy with the way things were going. But we were under no illusions: it would take a miracle to get him back to anywhere near his best.

I began to think about a target for him. We had to have something to aim at or things would drag on for ever and we'd never discover if he was able to race again. I chose a high-class gig for his comeback – the AIG (Europe)-sponsored Irish Champion Hurdle at Leopardstown, to be run towards the end of January 1996. This was the event in which he'd finished second to Fortune And Fame in 1994 and been forced to swerve the following year because of the cough.

My selection of this race provoked criticism – even an outcry. And sure enough, as it drew near, the flak began to fly. Everybody started getting worked up. All the gossip and rumours had said he'd never race again; now they were being forced to change their views. Reporters started to come then, and people wouldn't believe it when I said I was going to run him in the race. Many of them didn't agree with it, saying he'd never be the horse he was. Half of them didn't think I was telling the truth about running him.

There had to be a change of jockey, too. Since the Martell Aintree Hurdle, Charlie Swan had signed up with Aidan O'Brien and would have to ride Hotel Minella. So we put Tommy Treacy back on. The race came up and a television reporter asked me what I was expecting from Danoli. I said, 'If the horse is able to jump and stay with them for a mile and a half, I'm going to be thrilled.'

The pressure was intense and the thought of the first hurdle was really getting to me. So much so that I had to fight to keep control. The next thing the horse was walking around at the start and he and the rest of them were being brought under orders. I stood up and started praying. Really praying. My heart was pumping as they got to the first but he really pinged it and I remember thinking at the time, 'My prayers are answered.'

They started out along and he was lying up with the rest of them all the way. We were crossing the road at the far side with five or six furlongs to go and he was still up with the pace. I thought, 'I'm happy now. I don't care what happens as long as he's not hurt – he's been able to stay with them.'

But when they got to the third last, Danoli was there fighting it out with them for the lead. I just couldn't believe it and the tears started coming to my eyes.

I was after telling Tommy Treacy that day, 'Tommy, the minute he comes under pressure, just sit up on him. Don't ask him for an effort. Don't put the horse under any pressure whatever. For to get him back, that's all I want. This is one day the horse won't be put under pressure.' I could see Tommy sitting on the horse, trying to mind him and afraid to ask him the question. And we were still there knocking on the door and with a chance of winning the Champion Hurdle.

At the second last Danoli clipped the hurdle and lost some momentum, but he was soon back up with the leaders. They came to the last and there we were sitting in behind horses of the class of Collier Bay and Hotel Minella and you could sense he was fighting to do it.

You could see Tommy take out the stick and make a belt to hit the horse and him kind of saying, 'I don't want to hurt you.' Danoli was running on and running on and I reckon if it had been an extra furlong he'd have won it. As it was, he was beaten by just a head and half a length.

The crowd went mad and I did, too. We went down to the

winner's enclosure and everybody was shouting and yelling. I knew a lot of people were happy to see Danoli back, but I didn't realise the cheering was all for him. The winner, Collier Bay, came in followed by Hotel Minella, who'd finished second. There was a smattering of applause and that was it. But you wouldn't believe the roar that went up when Danoli came in and the crowd converged on him to a man. He'd lost, but in the hearts and minds of the racegoers he was the only winner. Collier Bay was standing there in the space reserved for the first, but no one went near him. No reporters or camera lads or anybody went over to him. They were all swarming round Danoli.

I felt sorry for Collier Bay that day – really, really sorry – because he was after winning a big hurdle race and we were after finishing third and no one was interested in him. Or jockey, Jamie Osborne, and trainer, Jim Old. And likewise Hotel Minella, Charlie Swan and Aidan O'Brien.

I wondered for a brief moment what was running through Charlie's mind as he saw the crowd mobbing the horse he'd abandoned. He must surely have wished he'd contracted with Aidan to stay on Danoli. Perhaps I'm wrong, but I can only assume he never expected Danoli to come back the way he did. We'd heard that's what he'd been saying to people, anyway. And if that was the case, fair enough; he's entitled to think and say what he likes. The way I look at it, though, is this: you can ride all the winners in the world, but you'll only ever ride one Danoli.

I hadn't time to dwell on Charlie, however. Danoli had run a huge race and it was a magical moment for me. To have him back the way he was and to see him putting in a performance like that was unbelievable. Just unbelievable.

The ovation he received – even in defeat – was the crowning glory for the People's Champion. I couldn't hold back the tears as I greeted him, for this was more emotional than any victory celebration. Charles Fawcus of the *Mirror* got it right when he wrote, 'Returning hero Danoli was given an Arkle-style reception – and he wasn't even the winner.'

Even the bookies were overwhelmed. Ladbrokes odds-maker, Mike Dillon, said: 'That was one of the greatest races I have ever seen anywhere in the world. Danoli is a truly remarkable horse. I'm making him joint favourite for the Smurfit Champion Hurdle at Cheltenham.' The paper were calling me a miracle-worker. They were talking about pilgrimages to Carlow. God knows what they'd have said if they'd known I'd put only two weeks of real, solid work into Danoli and that he hadn't jumped a single hurdle in preparation for the race. In fact he hadn't even looked at one since being injured at Aintree nine months earlier.

No, the miracle-worker was Danoli. He was the one with the gift. It took inborn talent, an iron constitution and extraordinary will-power to be able to return from such a lay-off. There was another factor: the horse just loves to race and he was back where he belonged. Perhaps he'd have won if he hadn't hit the second-last, or if Tommy had been allowed to get serious. But I didn't care. Getting round safely, not winning, was the objective. Everything else had been heaven-sent.

I'd had no sleep for a week but I made up for it that night. I was out as soon as my head hit the pillow. But I awoke next day with chants of 'Champion Hurdle, Champion Hurdle' in my head. We'd finished third to Alderbrook 12 months earlier and I was keen to have another go, particularly as Danoli had proved he was still up there. But before even thinking of the future, I wanted to see how he'd come out of the Leopardstown race. A performance like that can drain a horse and we knew after just a few days that he wasn't the same Danoli. He still wasn't able to eat and he hadn't bounced back like before. It took him that bit of time to come to himself.

Nevertheless, we had to press on with him and the Red Mills Trial Hurdle in Gowran was coming up. It was the only race we could go for before the Champion Hurdle and we decided to enter him. There were only three horses running against us, so we were certain we'd have to make it. Aidan O'Brien had pulled out Hotel Minella because of the testing ground, but he was pitching in his useful Tiananmen Square. He, like Danoli, had returned to action following a lay-off and was Cheltenham bound. I heard that Aidan and Charlie Swan were confident of beating us. I raised an eyebrow. Talk was cheap.

A crowd of 9,000 was crammed into the tiny ground and every vantage point around the paddock was taken long before the horses appeared. Racegoers clung to surrounding trees and perched on barbed wire fencing in the hope of seeing Danoli being paraded round the ring. I've never seen anything like it – not even for big races at Ascot or Newmarket. It was Gowran's own Cup Final, with a capacity crowd and an atmosphere to match.

Danoli would be wearing his lucky St Benedict medal sent by a Cork woman who'd told us she was praying for a miracle. She'd addressed the envelope simply 'Danoli' and the fact it reached us at all proved she could work them. The St Benedict medal, then, just had to go on the horse and I pinned it to the bridle. Fans had sent us statues, holy water and miraculous medals, too, to aid Danoli's recovery. One sent a statue of St Martin de Porres which I placed on a shelf over Danoli's box. Unfortunately it got blown down in the wind and the head broke off. Some would say that's good luck and who am I to argue?

Meanwhile the biggest miracle of all, Danoli, had entered the parade ring to a deafening ovation. He was cheered and applauded the whole way round and not until Tommy Treacy had been given the leg up on the horse and began making his way to the start did they rush away to watch the race.

Danoli went off a 2-5 shot and Tommy took him straight into the lead. The plan was to set a steady pace and keep increasing it to draw the finishing sting from Tiananmen Square, who'd be trying to do us for toe in the closing stages. I'd been a bit worried about making the running because of the way Danoli tends to idle in front, but Tommy seemed comfortable on him and I was pleased to see the tempo quicken as they headed towards the back straight.

Strangely, the ground was as quiet as a funeral. It was as if nobody in the packed stands dared utter a sound that might distract Danoli. Coming to the third last, Tiananmen Square and Jupiter Jimmy were closing ominously and Tommy began pushing for all he was worth. Danoli must have heard the others coming, because he responded immediately. He landed two lengths clear of Tiananmen Square over the second last and pulled away gradually to win by eight lengths. The roars of the crowd rang out at last from every enclosure and accompanied him all the way to the line as Tommy punched the air in celebration.

The stampede was on for the winner's enclosure and the cheer that went up when Danoli was led in would make you believe he'd won the Champion Hurdle. Of course, I was delighted with the sheer joy he'd inspired in racegoers since his comeback. As Michael Clower wrote in *The Sporting Life*: 'Not even Dawn Run inspired such affection. Indeed, no horse has caught the imagination of the Irish racing public like this since Arkle.'

I was still concerned that he wasn't the horse he was. He'd lost a bit of condition; each race seemed to be taking a little bit more from him. Yet he was happiest when he was racing and he was using the joint a lot more. It was getting stronger with each race.

So we started getting ready for Cheltenham. The sad thing was that we couldn't train him the way we did before. We used to do hill work and lots of it, but that was out. We did roadwork with him, too, but this time he hated it. He'd start getting worked up and pawing the ground and you knew the joint was paining him. We had to take him home.

It wasn't the best of preparations and, to make matters worse, we got real 'cat' ground. Thanks to a deluge of rain, the going changed overnight from good to very soft and ruined any chance we might have had of winning.

I could see after just two hurdles that Danoli didn't like the sodden turf. He wasn't striding out or jumping as well as I'd have liked, although I knew he'd run till he dropped.

The front-running Mysilv had blazed her usual trail. She was joined by Collier Bay at the top of the hill, with champion Alderbrook beginning to thread his way through the field. Danoli was tracking the front pair but a mistake two out, when they quickened, put paid to his hopes. Mud-lover Collier Bay stole a march on the rest of the field and went on to win from Alderbrook, with Pridwell finishing third to deny us the position we'd occupied twelve months earlier.

I wasn't too disappointed, considering the state of the ground. I'd known with a circuit to go that it wouldn't be our day and thought Danoli ran a great race to finish fourth.

We had him entered for the Martell Aintree Hurdle, the race that started all his problems the previous year. We thought we'd run him because it would be his last race for the season and a hat-trick in the Martell would have been some record.

So we went to Aintree and he was expected to win. He was 5-2 favourite but didn't jump well that day. The reason was that he was just too weak. By his own standards, he ran flat and was off the bridle most of the way. He failed to pick up but plugged on gamely to finish third, beaten a neck and six lengths by the Aidan O'Brien-trained Sun Alliance winner Urubande and the long striding Strong Promise.

So Charlie Swan had recorded a hat-trick of wins in the event, having piloted Danoli to victory twice previously. Knowing Charlie as I do, I don't think he'd have drawn comfort from beating him into third. He probably felt – in common with others – that the horse was just a shadow of his former self. By my rights, though, third place in a race like the Martell was creditable. And whereas people thought Danoli would never recapture his sparkle, I knew it was down to the fact he couldn't eat. It was a problem we hoped would resolve itself.

My concerns about his loss of condition had proved well founded. He needed more time now to recover between races and four outings in little more than two months had been enough for him. He needed a breather and we packed him off to Danny's for the summer.

Between then and the following season, a decision had to be taken as to whether he'd be sent chasing or stay hurdling. The thinking among most people was that we should keep him as he was because the leg wouldn't bother him as much over hurdles as over fences. But I couldn't see why jumping fences should be any different to jumping hurdles. So we took the decision that, if he adapted to fences, we'd go chasing with him. When he returned from Danny's place, we started his preparation. We got him good and fit, but the ground was too firm and we couldn't jump him.

Then a handy type of race came up at Clonmel at the beginning of November. The trouble was that, with only a week to go, Danoli had yet to jump a fence in anger. So I took him down to Ger Hourigan's place at Carrick-on-Suir in County Tipp, about a dozen or so miles from Clonmel. He and Lucy had sent a nice little card to Danoli when he got injured, with a touching message in it, saying, 'Get better soon, Danoli. You're much too nice to be laid up.' Ger (no relation to Michael) had three fences rigged up at home and the ground there had a bit of cut in it. So we thought we'd pop Danoli over them a few times. He jumped them all, no bother, and I was happy for him to run in Clonmel.

It was to be the start of a new career for Danoli. If he could do half as well at chasing as he'd done over hurdles, he'd make them all sit up and take notice.

But things didn't go quite to plan . . .

11

I'll Never Ask Charlie Again

WE went to Clonmel confident Danoli would soar to great heights. His coat looked a picture and I swear I could see my face in it. It was a sign he was back on song.

What a scene: the now usual huge crowd, a buzz in the air and Ireland's top racing reporters ready to tell the tale.

Then what happens? Just when you think nothing can go wrong, the roof caves in again. The death of Moon Man at Navan a year earlier almost to the day knocked me back, but I'd got over it well – or as well as anybody can get over something like that. I'd been helped by the miraculous recovery of poor old screwed-together Danoli and the emergence of another four-year-old prospect, Oxford Lunch.

An Oxford Lunch is a rich fruit cake, so you won't be surprised that the horse was owned by a firm of bakers, Comerford Brothers of Newbridge, Kildare. I rated him highly. He hadn't the class of Moon Man, but he was extremely useful - I could almost say tasty – and had a bright future as a hurdler.

We had him in an earlier race that day at Clonmel, but he was brought down when a loose horse ran across him. He looked none the worse, but Tommy Treacy injured his shoulder when he hit the ground and was unable to grab hold of the rein. Oxford Lunch got up and decided he'd run his race anyway. He jumped safely the whole way round but then he came up to the end of the race and thought he'd jump the white rail. Whatever way he met it I don't know, but he skewed over and broke a leg.

It shatters you when a horse is put down, regardless of its class. Oxford Lunch was no exception. In addition to your own pain, you have the owners to consider. Often it's the loss of a much-loved member of the family. For others, it's the end of a dream. In some cases both.

It happened that on this particular day, I'd have little time for my own or anybody else's feelings. Apart from being shaken at the fate of Oxford Lunch, I was concerned about Tommy. He looked as if his collar-bone was out, and I'd need a new jockey for Danoli. Either that or pull him out of the race.

Of course, there'd be a lot of people giving out that it was unfair to the public who'd paid to see him run. And I hated letting anybody down, particularly Danoli's devoted fans. My mind was in turmoil. On the one hand it was still spinning over the death of Oxford Lunch; on the other it was wrestling with the rights and wrongs of scrubbing Danoli.

My main worry was that this was Danoli's first chase. He'd only been popped over the odd few fences and with a new jockey up he, too, could fall and kill himself. I wasn't willing to take that chance. Suddenly, I realised the answer was staring me in the face. Charlie Swan was due to partner Consharon in the race, but he knew Danoli well – in fact, better than anybody. I went straight up and asked if he'd change horses. He said he'd have to get clearance from Aidan O'Brien, who was at Ballydoyle, and I left him to it. I didn't anticipate any problems.

So I could hardly believe my ears when Charlie turned me down. He said he'd phoned Aidan and been told that the owner wanted him to ride Consharon: 'I have to be loyal to the stable. I can't get off. I have to stay on Consharon.'

This was only a minor race, a novice event worth £2,500 to the winner. With respect to the sponsors, it meant little for any of the other runners in the way of prestige; but for a high-profile horse like Danoli, running for the first time over fences, it might as well have been the Grand National.

Danoli had given Charlie some of his greatest moments in racing – big wins at Cheltenham and Aintree, the showcase venues for National Hunt horses and jockeys. It took some believing that he was rejecting the chance to write himself another piece of history with the horse. I've heard what I'm supposed to have said to Charlie that day at Clonmel. So I'll put the record straight and tell you what I *didn't* say.

I didn't tell him: 'In future you won't even ride goats for me.' It may be amusing, but I didn't say it. I'll tell you exactly the words I used. I said: 'You're a shower of bollixes, the two of you (meaning him and Aidan O'Brien). You're not sportsmen at all.' I didn't say anything to him after that. It was all in the heat of the moment and I got a bit steamed up when he wouldn't switch rides. But I meant no harm by it and Charlie didn't have a go back at me. He just told me that his hands were tied and that it was down to the owner. I accepted what he said and left it at that, although I didn't like it one bit.

The Press lads were trying to help out by discovering if there were other jockeys available. They knew I was at the stage where I'd have to pull the horse out and were doing their best to prevent it happening. Like everybody else, they wanted to see him run. There were some big names there, like Tony O'Hehir, the *Racing Post* correspondent and RTE commentator, and Damien McElroy of the *Irish Independent*. They suggested I put up Philip Fenton.

He was a top amateur with a reputation for getting horses to jump. They'd tipped him off that he might be needed and he was hanging around, just in case. He sounded ideal for a horse like Danoli in his first chase.

By this stage, time was getting short and I was running out of options. So I asked Philip if he was available. He said he was and off he dashed to get changed.

The race was the London Heathrow Captain Christy Beginners' Chase over two-and-a-half miles. Danoli had 14 fences to jump and Philip followed my instructions to the letter. He held him up early on and moved gradually through the 12-runner field to go third at the eighth. By the tenth he was disputing the lead and after the next – the third from home – he let Danoli bowl along in front, finally pushing him out to win by six lengths from . . . who else but Consharon?

I was most impressed, both with horse and rider. Danoli had come through his first test over fences in impressive fashion. And Philip had made the most of his opportunity with a stylish and disciplined performance in the saddle. Philip's a pretty cool customer who rides work for Edward O'Grady, but for an amateur like himself to have landed a spare ride on a horse like Danoli must have been a dream come true:

> 'I didn't know I'd be riding Danoli until half an hour before the race. I'd never sat on him before and I was conscious of the fact that there was a big crowd at Clonmel to see him. I'd been told to stay handy because Tom Foley might have me in mind for the ride. So I waited around. Sure enough Tom asked me and I said, 'Fair enough. Let's go and get ready.'
>
> 'I was under a fair bit of pressure, but it helped that the race was so near. It meant I didn't really have time to think about it or the horse. When I got up on Danoli, he was fairly buzzing – you know, he was keen to get on with it. He came to the top

of the hill okay but coming back down I had to keep hold of him. To be honest, I rode him just like I'd ride any other horse. Tom had told me to pop him out handy and just get him jumping rather than give him a beating and maybe knock him or something. My instructions mainly were to get the horse round and to think about winning it after that.

'He jumped the first four fences okay and then he started to fiddle a little bit; but I was happy to let him fiddle because he was pretty good at it and it was just a novice chase. In the end he won it pretty easily and I was very happy. The pressure was off and to have ridden him for the first time and won on him was, obviously, a grand result. I'd describe him as a real tiger of a horse – the type who never knows when he's beaten. He's always alive with you. I knew it was just a one-off and that as an amateur I could never keep the mount. But it was a great thrill to partner him. I'm delighted to have been given the opportunity.'

I was just as delighted – and relieved – as Philip. After the shock of losing Oxford Lunch and the knock-back from Charlie, it gave me a tremendous lift to see Danoli jump round and beat Consharon the way he did. I wouldn't have been human otherwise. Emotions do play a part and I'm no different to anybody else in that respect.

I wasn't acting smug and I wasn't gloating. That wouldn't have been right and, in any case, I'm not made that way. But you can't help your feelings when a horse who has become so much a part of you starts his chasing career on such a high note. Especially when the man who's just turned down the chance of riding him comes trailing in second.

I didn't say anything to Charlie after we'd won, but I did make a point of seeing Consharon's owner, John Doherty, and asking him: 'Is it possible you wouldn't let Charlie off to ride Danoli?'

He said: 'What are you talking about?'

I repeated what Charlie had told me and he said: 'I never heard a word about it. I was never asked.

Blame was being passed around and in effect they were all saying, 'It wasn't me.' So whose decision it had been in the end I just don't know. And afterwards I wasn't too worried. But I got some thrill when the horse turned out and won so easily.

I'd been hoping that with the success Danoli had given Charlie over the years – he'd won seven out of ten on him, with two seconds and a third – he'd have got off the other one and ridden him for that reason alone. But it didn't work out that way.

Charlie's now saying he didn't want to disappoint the owners and that it wouldn't have looked too well for him if he'd switched mounts and Consharon had won. In other words, he had insufficient faith in Danoli. But his plea of 'stable loyalty' doesn't sound that logical to me and I didn't buy it as a reason. If that's what he meant, why did he get off Aidan O'Brien's Theatreworld in the Champion Hurdle at Cheltenham to ride I'm Supposin, a horse from Kevin Prendergast's stable that he'd never won a race on or even sat up on before?

Theatreworld had been his horse: he'd won good races on him. Yet he walked away from him. The fact Theatreworld finished second at Cheltenham and I'm Supposin could finish only fourth is neither here nor there. The point is, he could get off an Aidan O'Brien horse in a big race at Cheltenham and yet he couldn't get off an Aidan O'Brien horse to ride Danoli in a small race in Clonmel. It doesn't add up.

Whatever people want to make of it all is up to them. But I've presented the facts and no one can deny them.

About two-and-a-half months later, when Danoli fell at Leopardstown, it was suggested I'd asked Charlie to school the horse. But that's not true. I didn't ask him and there was never a mention of it.

I want to make it clear that I'm not anti-Charlie Swan. I won't pretend we're the best of friends, either, but if I met him in the morning, at least we'd stop and chat away. If you don't agree with somebody, it doesn't mean you have to fall out with them.

Basically I feel he wasn't very true to a horse that had given him a great deal of pleasure, for I reckon Charlie got a bigger kick out of riding Danoli than any other horse. He's said many times that he's one of the best he's ridden. And he admits that the highlight of his career was the day he won the Sun Alliance on him at Cheltenham. I know that because it's all in a book:*

> 'We hit the front at the top of the hill, the point furthest from the stands, and as we did so I could hear – even from that far away – a huge roar go up from the crowd. It was the Irish calling us home!'

Danoli fought off first Dorans Pride – who, as we know, fell at the last – and then Corrouge to win by two lengths. Charlie reckoned:

> 'It was a great performance by the horse and it triggered the most amazing scenes. All the way down the chute in front of the stands from the course to the unsaddling enclosure there were waves of Irish punters running down to the rail to cheer us in . . .
>
> '. . . We were mobbed all the way through the parade ring to the unsaddling area – scenes very reminiscent of Dawn Run's Gold Cup in 1986 and certainly the most fantastic reception I've ever known . . . Tom Foley was hoisted on to punters' shoulders, and it was impossible at that time to have even a brief conversation with him about how the race had gone. Amazing scenes!
>
> 'Every Cheltenham winner brings a fantastic buzz, but this

*_The Race Of My Life_, compiled by Sean Magee (Headline, 1996)

was very special indeed – and definitely the best experience of my riding life.'

There you have it, in his own words – the thrill and excitement Charlie got from riding Danoli. You'd have thought he'd give anything to stay riding a horse like that for the remainder of its career. Now, perhaps, you can understand my disbelief at his decision to turn his back on him in the hour of his greatest need. He knows in his heart and soul the way he stands in it with me, but he won't come out and say anything against me in any way. In fact, we both know where we stand.

In case you're confused, he's ridden horses for me since he last rode Danoli, even since getting off him in the Irish Champion Hurdle (to ride Hotel Minella). But not since he turned him down at Clonmel. *And that's the way it will stay.* When a lad turns you down once he doesn't get a second chance, unless he has a really good reason. And I reckoned his reason wasn't good enough that day.

Obviously if Danoli was running tomorrow and Danny O'Neill came up to me and said, 'I want you to put Charlie Swan up on him', I'd have to swallow hard and do it. It's the owners that decide who rides the horses I have here and that's the way it should be. But I know Danny feels the same as me about it. He was disappointed Charlie turned down Danoli. He's said to me a good few times that there's no way he'd want to see him riding the horse again. And I reckon he'd stand by that.

When Charlie was signing up with Aidan O'Brien, he said he'd have it written into his contract that he'd be free to ride Danoli when the horse returned from injury. But he didn't have it written in, or do anything about it – perhaps he didn't think Danoli would come back the way he did. That's how he came to be riding Hotel Minella against him at Leopardstown. Charlie's not stuck for good rides, but some horses really get through to you and you feel an obligation to them. I always would to Danoli, that's for sure.

For example, I wouldn't swap him for the Gold Cup winner or even the winner of the Derby. And neither would Danny O'Neill. I wouldn't even take him out of the box. I feel that strongly about him. He's done a lot for me and nobody would ever come between us. He'd never be second best to anybody where I'm concerned.

I've very few enemies in racing, thanks be to God. I like beating everybody, but I never mind when I get beat. I've nothing against any of them and I've nothing against Charlie Swan. He has his job to do and I have mine. And if things didn't work out between us, it's the way it goes. He's a real nice fellah. If I rang him in the morning and asked him to declare a horse for me, he's the very first person who'd do it.

In fact, he passed us on the way to Fairyhouse once and realised we'd have only five or six minutes to declare our horse. And that if we were held up, we might not even have that. The moment he got there he went over to the yoke, looked up the racecard to see what horse we were running and declared it. He had everything done for us by the time we went in.

I thanked him and he said to me, 'Any time – I'll help out any time. Just give me a ring.'

And I'd do the same for him. I wouldn't want people to think we're at loggerheads. It's just that we had a disagreement. I've met him several times since and there's never been a problem.

You'd find very few to say a bad word about him. He helps out lots of people. When Adrienne was making her debut as a rider, he was the very first to go to her – anything she wanted to know, he'd tell her; anything she wanted him to do, he'd do it. That's the type of man he is.

Going back to that day in Clonmel, I was vexed – that's the way. If he'd been riding one of the stars of the stable, I could understand it. But without being disrespectful to John Doherty, I found it hard to believe he was turning down Danoli to stay on

Consharon. If the two of them came into ratings in a handicap, Danoli would be conceding Consharon about four stones. And that's the difference.

When Charlie was riding for Edward O'Grady, he made a commitment that if he got the ride on Danoli in the 1994 Irish Champion Hurdle, he'd stay with him. You'll remember my having to tell Tommy Treacy that he'd lost the ride. It was a hard thing to do.

Well, Charlie did stay with Danoli until the horse got hurt at Aintree. And we never had a disagreement. He rode the horse 110 per cent every time, right and all. There was never a problem.

It was his decision – through 'stable loyalty' – to sever the partnership when Danoli made his comeback in the 1996 Irish Champion Hurdle. It was his decision at Clonmel – again through 'stable loyalty' – not to climb back aboard the horse who had given him 'the best experience of my riding life.'

He may regret it. For Danoli, the best is yet to come.

12
Gold Strike in the Hennessy

THE transition had been made from hurdles to fences. To the trainer, a small step of the imagination. To the horse, a giant leap into the unknown. To the jockey, um, hold on tight and keep the faith.

We decided we'd go for a race in Naas just eight days after Clonmel. Normally, I wouldn't run a horse twice like that, especially one starting out over fences; but, in all honesty, Danoli's chasing debut and the row surrounding it had taken more out of me than it had him. And I was keen to get another run into him before going for a valuable event at Fairyhouse at the beginning of December.

Thankfully, Tommy Treacy's shoulder injury wasn't as bad as first feared and the doctor gave him the all-clear.

The race was the Quinns of Naas Novices' Chase, worth £4,795 to the winner, and I can't pretend it was the greatest line-up ever seen. We were worried about a couple of suspect jumpers in it, the going was soft and we wanted to teach Danoli a thing or two. So we decided to pop him out last and settle him at the back of the field. It's not Danoli's way of running, but his starting price of 2–7 said everything and we were afraid a horse might fall and bring us down.

It wasn't until five out that he began to pick them off and Tommy didn't push him along until after they'd jumped the third last. Pace-setter Crossfarnogue stretched away just before the straight but had no answer to Danoli's class and was collared after the last. Danoli went away to win by two-and-a-half lengths.

That was chase win number two under our belts, yet the Press lads were critical of Danoli's performance. I couldn't work out why. We'd given horses in it 15 lengths and enough in a two-mile race on sticky ground and ended up winning comfortably. I was quite happy with the way he went.

So, as planned, we put him in the race at Fairyhouse – the Chiquita Drinmore Novices' Chase over two and a half miles. It attracted a top-class field including our old friend Dorans Pride, now also chasing the Gold Cup rainbow, and See More Business, a useful six-year-old trained in the west of England by Paul Nicholls.

The racing world was saying that this was make or break for Danoli as a chaser, but I didn't see it that way. Certainly it was his toughest test over the larger obstacles but, whatever happened, he'd learn from it.

I might have expected it to be a tactical contest and that's how it turned out. With the eight runners watching each other like hawks, the race didn't get going at all; there was a muddling pace on and Danoli began messing about. He's the biggest messer going when the pace doesn't pick up and, of course, he started looking around at the other horses and taking in the scenery, as if he was out somewhere for a hack canter. He didn't take a bit of notice of the third fence, hit it taking off and couldn't get the landing gear down. Result? He went over on top of his head.

The race was won by Dorans Pride, with Richard Dunwoody up. He got home by a length from See More Business, who'd given Tony McCoy a bumpy ride by going through the top at a couple of fences.

So what next for Danoli? By all accounts, his career over fences was dead and buried. The obituaries had been written. Only the inquest remained. The verdict: Fallen by the wayside. The advice: go back to hurdling. Now I've been called a miracle-worker, but I needed to produce another one if I was to believe everything that was being said. I wasn't sure about miracles but I was determined to show one or two people. I was pleased, then, that I'd taken the opportunity to school Danoli after racing at Fairyhouse. There's no better tonic than to pop a faller straight back over a few fences; it helps restore confidence. And I knew by the end of the session that there was nothing wrong with Danoli's mind or his jumping.

There was a real nice race – the Denny Gold Medal Chase – coming up at Leopardstown on Boxing Day. It was worth £22,750 to the winner and provided me with the perfect opportunity to make Danoli's critics eat their words. This is not meant in a malicious way; but any kind of unfair criticism gets to me and I have to prove people wrong. So I concentrated on giving Danoli some speed work to sharpen him up. He was already fit enough by now and our efforts in getting him to increase his intake of food were beginning to pay off. He was up to 15lb a day – still way short of what he was consuming before his injury, but it was a struggle we appeared to be winning.

What with Christmas on the way and cards and presents to buy, the holiday racing programme comes at the wrong time of year for National Hunt trainers and jockeys – especially the jockeys, who have to monitor their weight. It's okay for all those Flat race lads swanning off to exotic places like Barbados or the Seychelles, wherever that is. But this is one of the busiest times of the year for us and we wouldn't have it any other way. On top of everything else, there's all the feasting and merry-making – and the recovering afterwards. It's a tough life. Then, of course, there are the horses to train and groom so that they're looking and running their best over the holiday. Thanks to Goretti and the girls and our hard-working stable staff, we seem to manage. But it's important not to forget what it is we're celebrating and going to Mass with the family on Christmas day to offer praise for all we've been given is, to me, the most gratifying part of it all.

No National Hunt trainer with good horses in the yard would want to miss the holiday meetings. Competition is fierce, yet a wonderful peace and calm pervades the whole racing scene. And the huge, cheery crowds that turn out make the whole exercise worthwhile. Danoli, oddly enough, had never won over the Christmas period. The previous year he was recovering from injury. In 1994 he'd had the cough. And the Christmas before he'd been beaten into third place in the 1st Choice Novice Hurdle. This time, though, I had him pretty well spot-on.

He'd need to be because there was a real tough horse over from England for the race – Paul Webber's useful Land Afar, to be ridden by Jamie Osborne. This one had proved more than a match for the best and Jamie wasn't coming over to sample the breeze blowing in off the Liffey. A six-year-old of Arthur Moore's, Jeffell, was also strongly fancied. The race appeared to be between the three of us. That's how it looked on the bookies' boards, anyway, with Danoli and Jeffell going off joint 5–2 favourites and Land Afar next best at 3–1. But they might just as well have been 100–1 shots for all the chance they stood.

I'd told Tommy to ride a much more attacking race than at Naas, where the object had been to educate the horse over fences. And, sure enough, he had Danoli well up with the pace as Crossfarnogue, whom he'd beaten at Naas, went off in the lead. Danoli, wouldn't you know it, made a blunder at the fourth and my blood pressure shot up. But I wasn't too bothered. I could see he was full of himself and I knew that once Tommy let him go he'd take some beating.

We were in front sooner than expected when Crossfarnogue crashed out at the sixth. Beakstown tried to go with us, but was fighting a losing battle. Neither he nor any of the others could match Danoli's pace once Tommy put him into overdrive after the second last. Danoli jumped the last cleanly and fairly sprinted clear to beat Land Afar by six lengths, the near-20,000 holiday crowd letting out a mighty roar throughout the final furlong as Tommy waved his whip in triumph.

Whenever the horse runs, it fills me with awe as I experience the joy and excitement felt by the public. Once again, the mad rush to the unsaddling enclosure to give him a hero's welcome proved just how much they adored him. They cheered him to the echo, bringing back memories of Cheltenham in the same way they'd done before at Leopardstown when Danoli made his emotional comeback. Rapturous receptions like these are rare indeed in racing and yet this latest was Danoli's third of 1996. The effect is always overwhelming; it's enough to make your heart burst with pride. The emotion wells up in you and you can't catch your breath. The tears flow and you can't stop them. You try to speak and no words come.

Yet if I'd followed the advice handed out after the fall at Fairyhouse just three weeks earlier, we wouldn't even have been at Leopardstown. We'd have been slinking off to obscurity. Again, if I'd taken notice of everything I'd heard or read since Danoli's injury, where would the horse be today? He'd have been retired prematurely, albeit to a life of plenty on Danny O'Neill's farm. And the pleasure he has brought and is bringing still to countless men, women and children – especially children – would have been lost. As it is, my faith in this horse has been rewarded many times over. They said he'd never race again and he did. They said he'd never make it to the top again and he did. They said he'd never jump fences and he did.

After this latest success at Leopardstown, however, everybody was united in agreement: Danoli would make a great chaser. But this horse who's so full of surprises had yet one more in store, although this time an involuntary one. Once again he would test the will and resolve of those who had doubted him.

We were now into 1997 and I'd decided on two more races at Leopardstown – the Baileys Arkle Perpetual Challenge Cup Chase over two miles, one furlong, and the three-mile Hennessy Cognac Gold Cup – as a prelude to a challenge for the Tote Gold Cup at Cheltenham. It was an ambitious programme, but I knew Danoli was up to it.

The Baileys Arkle, worth £9,675 to the winner, was down for decision in the third week in January. The pressure was on again, with an extremely smart horse called Mulligan, trained in England by David Nicholson, travelling across for it. That didn't worry me unduly because if we stood up we were going to be there with a chance. We were odds-on favourite at 9-10, with Mulligan at 2-1, and I believe it was a fair reflection of how the race should finish. Aidan O'Brien's Penndara was also in the field, with Charlie Swan up. They were rank outsiders at 20-1 and presented little threat on the evidence of their tailed-off seventh in the Denny Gold Medal.

We jumped off on the outside, cleared the first fence and everything seemed grand. Penndara was on the inside, with the Adrian Maguire-ridden Mulligan between the two of us and yet slightly ahead. Mulligan went a few lengths up coming to the second, with Penndara still on the inside, just in front of us. Mulligan jumped the fence well but Penndara veered to the right where we were and jumped sideways all across us. Danoli was about to take off, found there was no room for him to jump and made a mess of things. As he couldn't jump over the fence he had no option but to jump into it and he toppled over as a result.

It's on the record that Danoli fell that day. I say we didn't fall. I say Penndara got in our way and brought us down. Some horses have the characteristic of jumping to the right or to the left at fences and Penndara, it seems, is one of them. He certainly did us no favours.

It's very easy for one horse to distract another and there's no way I'd blame Charlie; he couldn't do a lot about it. He wasn't brought in by the stewards and questioned about the incident and therefore he did nothing wrong. You can't say anything against him in that line. But when you've been riding as long as he has, you pick up things that help you along the way. They say it's the hard dog for the long road and it's all part of the art of race riding.

Charlie's no different to Adrian Maguire or Richard Dunwoody or any of the rest of them. They've all done things in their time that other jockeys didn't like: that's the way it is. Look at how Henry Cecil gave out about Mick Kinane's riding at Ascot. He reckoned Mick had 'squeezed up' his stable jockey, Kieren Fallon. And that's putting it mildly. The papers were full of it.

Race riding is a tough business. There's no quarter asked or given. You go down to the start of a race and hear the jockeys giving out and cursing at one another. Listen to them during a race and you'll hear them cursing each other for cutting in front or barging their way through. Then they come back in and they're all pals: they just say those things in the heat of the moment.

If you're a jockey you want to win because that's how you make your name. You don't make your name by getting beaten. You have to show by your determination that you want to win. But the way I saw it that day, Penndara had absolutely no chance of beating Danoli or Mulligan. So it was the greatest pity that he caused Danoli to fall and spoiled what I'm certain would have been a great contest with the English horse. A contest I'm certain Danoli would have won.

Penndara ran on to finish third behind Mulligan and Beakstown, beaten nine lengths and one length. But for Mulligan being eased right down near the finish, he'd have been even farther adrift.

The worst aspect was that people began running to Danny O'Neill and telling him Tommy was no good – that he had no idea how to ride the horse, that he was responsible for him falling and had no business riding him at all. But I knew Tommy wasn't at fault; he'd ridden Danoli as straight as a gun-barrel. And it was Danoli's own fault when he'd fallen at Fairyhouse. We decided to take no notice. Tommy would keep the ride.

We'd had two falls over fences – but there'd be no submission. The Leopardstown incident may have placed fresh doubts in people's minds, but I knew Danoli was a good jumper and I knew he was still a good horse. In fact, a great horse. So we stuck to our plan to run him in the Hennessy Cognac Gold Cup, to be run back at Leopardstown two weeks later. They don't come much bigger than the Hennessy or much richer, as underlined by the winner's prize of £62,500.

As you'd imagine, the race attracted the top chasers in Ireland and from across the water. The home challenge was spearheaded by Cheltenham Gold Cup winner Imperial Call, trained down in Cork by Fergie Sutherland, the Jim Dreaper trail-blazer Merry Gale and, of course, Danoli. The English invasion was led by Peter Beaumont's powerful veteran, Jodami, who'd taken this valuable race three times in as many attempts, Gordon Richards' classy nine-year-old, The Grey Monk, and the ex-Irish trained Belmont King.

People's memories are short in racing. You're only as good as your last success – or fall. And there were very few who thought we'd have the beating of Imperial Call, the even money favourite, or, for that matter, Jodami. Nevertheless, there was some money for Danoli at 6-1. It proved we weren't exactly friendless in the market.

We did our homework on the way the race was likely to be run. Merry Gale was a strong front-runner, fast and fluent at his fences. It would be tough matching him stride-for-stride from the off. I reckoned Merry Gale would probably lead to the third last where, with any luck, we might be able to take it up.

I was around the stable yard before the race and Jim Dreaper, the trainer of Merry Gale, came down. He's a very straight and decent fellow and Richard Dunwoody was riding his horse that day.

I asked him: 'Are you going to try and make it with Merry Gale?'

He said: 'Well, I don't mind. He doesn't mind being up there. Yeah, I wouldn't mind making it if no one else does. But Richard Dunwoody's after telling me The Grey Monk is going to make it.'

I thought to myself, 'Two good jumpers. If we try and make it and take on Merry Gale and The Grey Monk, they'll possibly knock us back.'

I had a good discussion with Tommy, during which I decided to put my fears to one side: we'd go out and have a go at making it after all. I told Tommy that if by any chance Merry Gale and The Grey Monk stayed with us, to make sure he kept a length off them. Otherwise Danoli might try to match their stride pattern at the fences and come to grief.

So, begod, we jumped off anyhow and it ended up that we were out in front, with Merry Gale and The Grey Monk following and trying to keep up with us! We led them over the first but, coming to the second, Merry Gale jumped up and joined us. He then went on in front. So Tommy sat back and did everything right – he let him get on with it and took a tow behind. But after jumping the fifth, I think it was, The Grey Monk came up with us as well. Then, at the seventh, Danoli went between the two of them and decided he'd go on. He passed Merry Gale and got away from him and started to make it, with The Grey Monk in close attendance.

They battled on together and came to the fence where Danoli was brought down in the Baileys Arkle – it was the second then but, this being a three-miler, I'm not sure what it was this time. I was kind of getting nervous at that stage as to what would happen at the fence and whether it might trigger his memory. But he jumped it grand, no problem.

Then it was hell for leather with the two of them all down the back straight. Our fellah made a bit of a mistake and Tommy gave him a tip with the stick to remind him. It woke Danoli up and he realised that things were different this time. Coming to the sixth last, Tommy really asked him for a big one. The Grey Monk decided to try and jump with him but at the last moment he must have thought, 'No, I can't take off from there' and kind of put back down again. He ended up on the back of his head with his jockey, Tony Dobbin, going out the side door.

Danoli was left in front but it wasn't long before Imperial Call joined him and took him on. He outjumped Danoli at the next and we thought we were in trouble. It seemed as if Imperial Call would draw away from him. So, begod, come the next fence, Danoli outjumped Imperial Call and got back in front. The heat was on and the two of them were fighting it out coming to the second last. Danoli jumped it well and so did Imperial Call, but Danoli got away from it quicker and Imperial Call came under pressure.

Danoli began to stretch clear of him, as if he'd decided, 'I've let this fellah tag along – now he can get lost.' And it just so happens that this 'fellah' was the Cheltenham Gold Cup winner.

Then Jodami started after us with one of his usual thundering great runs and it seemed he was making up ground. We were getting kind of nervous. I thought that if we could just get over the last, Jodami would have his work cut out to pass us.

So Danoli came to the last. He stood off and pinged it and they started on the long run for home. Jodami made progress for a while, but that was it: he was getting no closer. Danoli kept finding that little bit more; he knew it was his day and that he was going to win it. And sure enough he kept galloping strongly to the line, with Tommy standing up in the irons to acclaim the victory.

I was overjoyed. We'd kept faith with the horse and kept faith with Tommy and this was the result – a glorious triumph that sent the huge crowd wild with delight. I was particularly thrilled for Tommy after the stick he'd taken; and I was thrilled for Danny O'Neill. The prize-money had upped Danoli's career earnings to a colossal £320,759. That's some recompense for the decision Danny took some years back never to sell the horse. And, of course, I was thrilled with Danoli himself. Once again he'd weaved his magic spell over Leopardstown and the reception he received from the 18,000 crowd – a record for the Hennessy – had to be seen and heard to be believed.

The scenes that follow his victories are equally fantastic but, at the same time, they're all different and unique. The cheers and the tears – they go together. One inevitably follows the other and it's something I just can't hide. It's not the emotion of winning, because I'd call that jubilation and jubilation doesn't bring tears. It's the emotion of coming through against the odds and then receiving the kind of reception that defies belief. The best comparison I can draw is that this kind of adulation is normally reserved for rock stars and singers who touch people with their lyrics and the melody of their songs. Danoli's bravery whispers to their soul.

I hadn't realised the size of the crowd, but they started flooding into the unsaddling enclosure and fighting to get a glimpse of Danoli. I was jostled, patted, pushed and hugged and Tommy was waving and everybody was crying but Danoli. He was loving every minute.

As I started back with the horse to head down towards the stable yard, I sidled up to him and whispered to *his* soul. I said to him quietly: 'Danoli, I don't care if you never win another race this year or ever again. You've done everything I've asked and whatever you do from here on in is a bonus.' The nudge he gave me with his head convinced me he understood.

So now, in little more than a month, we'd be heading off to England for a crack at the Tote Cheltenham Gold Cup. And as long as he came home safe and sound, I'd be happy.

If ever a horse deserved to win it, for his own sake and for Ireland, it was Danoli. The People's Champion.

A Man's Best Friend. *(Daily Express)*

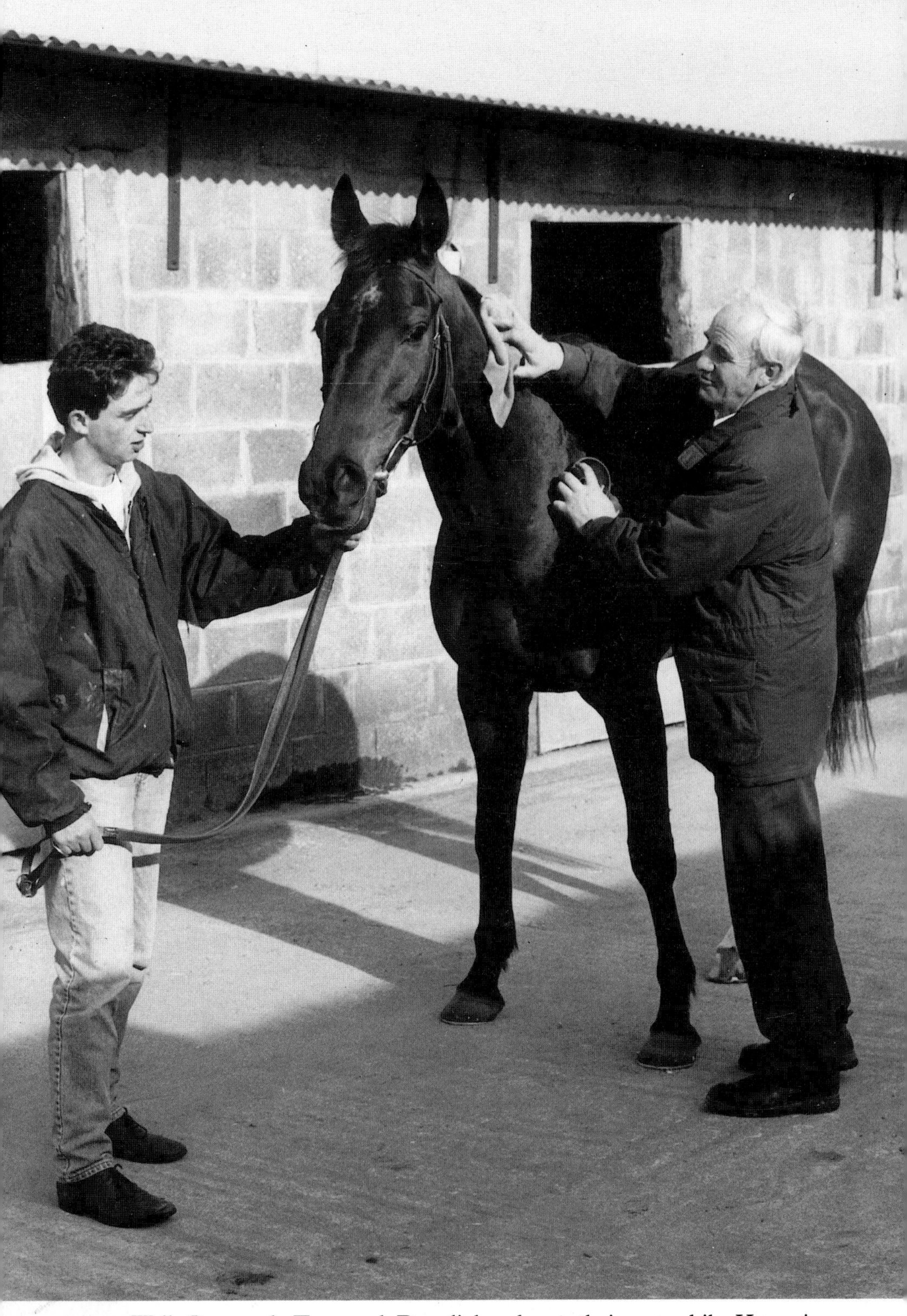

Well Groomed: Tom and Danoli brush up their act while Hammie Hamilton looks on.

Family Matters: Sharon, Goretti junior, Goretti, Pat, Tom and Adrienne Foley.

Class Act: The children of St Finian's wish Danoli well.

Gowran Glory: Crowds pack the parade ring to catch a glimpse of their hero before his victory in the Red Mills Trial Hurdle. *(Healy)*

That's My Boy: Tom Foley lifts young Paul Minchin to congratulate Danoli on his comeback victory after injury. *(Healy)*

No Surrender: Danoli gets the measure of Jodami in the Hennessy Gold Cup.
(Healy)

What a Welcome! Tom punches the air in celebration as Danoli is led in after winning the Hennessy Gold Cup. (Danny O'Neill, right, and Tommy Treacy, centre) *(Healy)*

King of the Hill: Danoli is monarch of all he surveys. *(Caroline Norris)*

13

Danny Boy has the Gift

'DANNY O'NEILL'S place? If I'd a pound for every time I've been asked that question, I'd be a rich man today.'

So speaks the polite man in the grocery store as he temporarily suspends the cutting of a succulent joint of best quality Irish ham into lean, thinly-cut slices and prepares to direct another stranger to the home of the 'luckiest person in Ireland.'

At least, that's how an increasing number of people have come to regard the owner of the great Danoli. It's not just the volume of the prize-money he has amassed, although, to any non-aligned neutral, a return of upwards of £320,000 (and still counting) on an original outlay of £7,000 cannot in any sense be considered bad business. And nor can it be considered an altogether trivial aspect of ownership, to be dismissed airily as coming a poor second to the chasing of 'The Dream' and the kudos of having a horse registered in your own name and colours. No. It's the sheer thrill of having sole proprietorial claim on a horse which can run like the wind even if, in the minds of the many, he has still to prove he can jump like a stag.

Danny's prized equine possession is looked upon with all the covetousness of a man sinfully lusting after his neighbour's wife. The Irish are born to a love of horses; they regard them with a passion that is unequalled anywhere in the world. It eclipses even their thirst for the black stuff. Well, almost.

The polite man in the grocery store is clearly of that persuasion. For they know the time of day in Myshall and, more particularly, the time of year. Cheltenham is just a week away and the village is beginning to stir from its gentle slumber beneath the foothills of Mount Leinster.

'Do you think Danoli can do it?' The question comes in hushed, conspiratorial tones, as if some top-secret mission that has been plotted for years is about to be unleashed on the unsuspecting English.

The polite man does not wait for a response. He has the answer all along. 'He'll win of course, God willing,' comes the soft, almost inaudible reply to his own question.

He ventures as far as the door and points. 'Now then, Danny O'Neill's: second turning on the left, come back slightly on yerself, and its the first entrance on the left.'

The directions are accurate, as somehow you never doubted they would be. But your stomach tightens as soon as you turn on to the 400-acre O'Neill estate. There on a board bang in front of you, writ large, are the unwelcoming words: PRIVATE – NO ENTRY. The polite man in the grocery store said nothing of this.

Only a brave man or a fool would soldier stoically on past such a blunt, unambiguous warning sign but the prize on offer – an audience with a man who famously enjoys the good fortune of being, at one and the same time, farmer, bone-setter and owner of Ireland's best-loved racehorse – seems worth the risk. So, like an intrepid explorer on a pioneering mission that must not fail, you disregard the notice and continue on resolutely through a narrow entrance bounded on either side by stark white-painted walls, half expecting as you emerge at the other end to be greeted by a warning blast from a shotgun. Or, at the very least, a pack of savage, snarling hounds scraping their claws down the pristine paintwork of your car.

Instead, what confronts you is a scene of idyllic splendour straight from the pages of *Country Life*: a substantial 200-year-old, 13-room granite house sitting atop a lush green landscape that stretches almost as far as the eye can see. And not a smoking gun or wild dog in sight.

Tess O'Neill, Danny's wife of many decades and mother of his seven grown-up children, bids you welcome to Hollybrook House. She is a dainty-looking woman, smartly turned out in patterned cotton dress and a pair of matronly specs perched neatly on her finely-chiselled nose – in short, about as far removed from the image of the archetypal farmer's wife as it's possible for a woman to be. Her slight, almost delicate build seems to fit her personality: her voice light and somewhat refined, her manner pleasing and friendly. You get to wondering how, not being a powerful wench of a woman, she managed to cope all those years with the rough-and-tumble of life on the farm: the feeding, the milking, the fetching and carrying, the rearing of a large family and, at one and the same time, being dutiful wife-cum-secretary to a husband whose legend somewhat preceded that of his horse. And you realise at once that beneath this deceptively fragile, almost diffident exterior is a woman of character and inner strength for whom the work ethic clearly held few terrors and system and order must overwhelmingly have won the day.

This is evidenced by the cleanliness and neatness of the house; everywhere is spotless, including notably the large country-style kitchen which, as in most Irish households, seems to act collectively as dining room, living room, office and family meeting point.

These days, of course, things are very much easier for Tess O'Neill. The children she struggled to rear are now young adults, Danny has made his pile and she and the family are incontrovertibly bound up in the celebrity brought to them by the unlikely ownership of a racehorse.

Tess has the kettle on and is busily tending to household matters while at the same time extolling the virtues of another horse – 'just a baby' – which she and her spouse have placed with Tom Foley. Of him, more later. Danny, she explains unapologetically, is 'messing around outside' and will be in shortly. He appears, finally, as if materialising before your very eyes, a broad, heavily-built man decked out in green wellies, a shock of white hair sprouting upwards from his dome and three small, startlingly white teeth standing stiffly to attention like sentries in his upper jaw.

He has a ruddy face, twinkling eyes and a genial manner very much at odds with the distinctly antisocial sign that warns off unwanted visitors to his property. At 67 he seems completely at ease with himself and life in general, his comfortable, relaxed persona reflecting perfectly his circumstances and surroundings.

This is a man who has achieved the rarity of dual celebrity status in Ireland, both for his prowess as a bone-setter – people come from as far afield as the United States to experience his healing touch – and his ownership of Danoli. The two go hand in glove, one reflecting his regard for humanity (he does not charge for his services, though people reward him generously) and the other his devotion to a horse.

His means are such that he has been able to turn his back on substantial offers for Danoli. He does not mention specific sums, but they were of the 'name your price' variety. He states emphatically that he'll never sell the horse and you believe him absolutely. You sense that to him it would be an act of unspeakable treachery, like selling off a member of the family.

He feels privileged to own a horse that has become not only a household name in Ireland but a national institution. That Danoli is unquestionably the country's most popular racehorse was confirmed by the screening during the 1997 Eurovision Song Contest in Dublin of footage of the horse at work and at play, filmed at Aughabeg in the busy run-up to Cheltenham.

The twin aim of state-owned programme makers Radio Telefis Eireann was to reflect to a viewing audience of 500 million the traditional image of Ireland as a horse-loving nation and the fact that the racing, breeding and bloodstock industry makes a significant contribution to the nation's economy. Some even say it underpins it. Danoli was chosen to symbolise this and, according to Danny O'Neill, it was perfect casting.

He was understandably flattered: 'For your horse to be chosen to represent the nation on television – and be seen by such a huge number of people – was just wonderful. It made us feel so proud.'

Pride is embedded deep in the O'Neill consciousness. Hitting the jackpot with his first racehorse, his prowess as a healer, his productive farm comprising cattle, sheep, tillage and horses, a loving and supportive family – all are sources of deep satisfaction. And he is especially proud of his roots.

His father, Dan, was a local man who, in common with countless others of his generation, decided temporarily to forsake jobless Ireland and seek his fortune across the Atlantic. He settled in New York, where he made money as a car-dealer and met and married Mary Brennan, a native of those parts. They had two children – Mary and Margaret – before leaving for a life of rural bliss in the country and county of his birth. Danny was born within a year of his parents' arrival. Then came another sister, Anne.

'My dad was one of 12 children,' says Danny. 'He was born in Ballinrush, just across the way, on the farm next to this one. He wasn't allowed to set foot on this place: every time they saw him, they ran him with dogs. This was before he went to America.

When he came home and heard the place was for sale, it gave him the greatest pleasure buying it. He paid £2,800, including the contents and everything else that went with it.

'Shortly after my parents arrived from America, my mother had quite a scare. She went down to post a letter. At that time you walked; there was no such things as cars. There was this eccentric old woman – she was very, very old – who used to go to Mass every morning. That day she stood outside praying for my mother. She called her over and said to her: "Mrs O'Neill, Mrs O'Neill – I don't want to upset you, but there was never a child born alive in that house. The last one flew out the window as a crow."

'It was 1929 and my mother was expecting me at the time. So you can imagine how she felt, fresh over from New York and being confronted with that kind of talk. She never let it worry her, but she must have wondered what she'd let herself in for.

'But all was well. I was born in the house and I didn't fly out the window as a crow, although I probably did my share of squawking. Now, of course, I'd be too big to fly out.'

Danny married Tess, a local girl from Ballyneen, three miles distant, in 1964. They have seven grown-up children: Dan (32), Mary (30), Jimmy (28), Gretta (26), Clare (24), Olivia (22) and Treasa (20).

'There's two years between each of them, so I've no trouble remembering their ages,' he chuckles. That's typical O'Neill. Timing is everything, as he proved with his purchase of Danoli.

'Mary has a house in Maynooth, where she keeps students. Gretta is teaching in Enniscorthy, Clare's nursing in England, Olivia's in the middle of a course on sports psychology and Treasa's doing languages at University College Dublin. The boys, Dan and Jimmy, are both farming.'

It was after Danoli had won the Sun Alliance Hurdle at Cheltenham in 1994 that life changed dramatically for the O'Neills. And particularly Danny.

'RTE did a programme on the horse,' he says. 'The background song they put to it was "Nobody Does It Better", by Carly Simon. It was a lovely piece – absolutely brilliant. It really got to me. I saw the RTE sports editor at Punchestown races sometime afterwards and thanked him. He asked how the horse was and said: "I've bad news for you. You don't own Danoli any more. He belongs to the people of Ireland." He went on to say that he'd never seen a horse the public had taken to so much and hoped I wouldn't sell him. I told him I'd *never* sell.'

Despite all the offers, Danny has remained steadfast. There's no doubt now that he'll remain so, but has he ever wavered?

'The nearest I ever came to selling him was the time soon after I bought him, when I could have doubled my money more or less straight away. I was over at Tom's just to take a look at him. Tom was working the horse at the time and he said: "If you want to sell him, I can double your money now. I might even get £15,000 for him. It's up to you."

'When you're talking about that kind of profit – £8,000 in just a few days – it needs thinking about. And that's all I did. Think about it.

'One day I mentioned over dinner that I could sell the horse for around £15,000. Tess said: "You'll do no such thing. You need something to get you out of that room down there. Whether he wins an odd race or whether he doesn't, we won't be broke. You're not to sell him." Thank God I didn't, because the horse has won £320,000 in prize money. Out of this, though, the trainer and jockeys each receive 10 per cent, the Turf Club made deductions for entry fees and the like and whatever was left went to me. It's all right for the likes of us with Danoli winning all that money, but I feel for owners of horses that just win an odd race here and there. It must be hard for them to stay in it with all those deductions.

'Then there's training fees and things like travelling expenses. Tom's very reasonable; his fees are only around £95 a week and if he takes a horse to a place like Leopardstown, he might charge something like £25. It would barely cover his costs, what with the price of diesel and the wear and tear on his car. Mind you, Toyota have given him a jeep for the year to go with their colour ads: DANOLI TRAVELS SMOOTHLY. So that should be a help to him.

'The money we've won with Danoli hasn't made a huge difference to our lifestyle, but it did enable us to buy a 62-acre farm at Rathrush, near Tullow, about a mile from another 100-acre farm we own at Bendenstown. It cost £180,000 and it had a bungalow on it, which Dan has converted into a two-storey house. He lives there with his wife, Bernie, and they presented us with our first grandchild last April. His name? I'll give you two guesses, but you'll need only one. Yes, they called him Danny.?

As Danoli effectively paid for the farm at Rathrush, it will bear his name. Fittingly, the plaque that's set into the wall at Hollybrook House, and which was sculpted from a photograph of the horse by a local firm of stonecutters, will be removed and erected there. But Danoli Farm will never have its famous benefactor stabled there. On his retirement, Danoli will live out his days with Danny and Tess on the farm at Myshall, where he spends his summers away from the rigours of racing.

The naming of the horse was an inadvertent master stroke by Danny. It could hardly have struck a more resonant chord with the public:

'We'd discussed it at some length, but couldn't make up our minds. Then one day I was out in the car with Olivia and we hit on the idea of using the first three letters of each of our Christian names, hence Dan-Oli. We pronounced it Dan-olly but the race commentator at Naas referred to him as Dan-owe-li and we decided to stick with it. A lot of people call him Danolly still.' Tess says: 'We thought Dan-owe-li sounded much better. It's got more of a ring to it.'

It's no surprise to learn that every member of the family is in love with the horse. Danny explains how Tess played a trick on their daughter, Clare, to test what her reaction would be if they sold Danoli.

'After his first season, Clare was nursing in Dublin and Tess went up to meet her. She said to her, "You'll miss Danoli now, won't you?"

'"Why? What do you mean?"

'"We've sold him. We've sold Danoli."

'"You have not!"

'"Well, we got £300,000 for him."

'Claire started to cry. "I'm not going home," she said. "It doesn't matter how much you got – you shouldn't have sold him." Tess put her arms round her and said: "I'm only codding you. We'd never sell him." That will tell you how members of the family would feel if we really did sell Danoli, even for that kind of money.

'It gives me a great buzz whenever I visit him down at Tom's place. He's marvellous. The year he won at Cheltenham, we were new to it all. We didn't realise what was happening. We look back at it on the tape and realise what that day really meant. And then Leopardstown the last time, when he won the Hennessy – the crowd went absolutely crazy.'

Danny's bone-setting gift has been in the family 400 years, being passed down through the generations. But it wasn't until he was 30 that he discovered he'd inherited it:

'My uncle Pat used to do it. He was pretty famous around these parts. His only child was a daughter who became a nun. Everybody thought it was the end of the line then, because my father couldn't do it. He'd tried a few times without success. After Pat died, an old fellah from Tullow rang up one time. He said his daughter was after falling and there was something wrong with her arm. I knew him well, very well. He asked if I'd have a look at her. I said, "I know nothing about it."

'I told him about another uncle and an aunt of mine who might be able to help him, but he said: "I don't know those people but I know you. Will you look at it for me anyhow?" I said, "I will, surely, only you're wasting your time coming out."

'So I looked at it and examined it and said: "I think the wrist is dislocated."

'He said: "If it is, put it back."

'I again mentioned my uncle and aunt, who lived 15 miles away, but he said: "You do it and don't let down the name. You're the only one left now and I'll not leave here till you try it."

'I said: "Fair enough. If you're prepared to chance it, I'll chance it; but don't blame me if it goes wrong."

'And he said: "It won't go wrong."

'So I felt the hand and gave it a bit of a twist. It flicked straight back in and he said: "Now can't you do it?"

'That was the beginning of it. It just took off from there. Word gradually got round. I carried on with the farming and worked late at night on the bone-setting, including working on the animals. It just so happened that the farming was getting easier. We had a tractor by then – a small Ferguson 20 – and it was *the* tractor that time. It meant I had time to devote to the bone-setting.'

The realisation that he possessed The Gift transformed Danny's life and circumstances. The magic hands that formerly worked on farm machinery were now working on human machinery. Here was the healer, the man who could banish pain and cure cripples. Life on the farm would never be the same again:

'It was a gift from God, no doubt about it. To have taken a hand and put back the wrist, having never seen or done anything like it before, was surely a blessing. I was seven or eight years at it, but I wouldn't look at backs. I was afraid of my life I'd do some harm. I wouldn't touch them.

'I was just up the hill from here one morning and this fellow stopped me. He said: "Jimmy's in the bed with a pain in the back and he can't get out of it. Maybe if you came in you might do something for him."

'I said, "I know nothing about backs. Can't he see the doctor?"

'"To hell with the doctor. He told him to stay in bed for three days. That was a fortnight ago. He's not a bit better; it's only worse he is."

'"Take him down to Jimmy Heffernan in Tipperary, then, for I know nothing about backs."

'"God damn it, aren't I tellin' you he can't move in the bed? Maybe if you came in you could do something for him. At least try and help him."

'So I went in. It was the middle of November and the wife was feeding him. He was in terrible pain – he couldn't move. We managed to turn him over and I began. Halfway up his back, I put my thumb on the spot and he yelled out: "Oh, Jaysus, that's where it is." I don't know what way it was, but I asked yer man to lift up his leg and pull it back and I felt something go. I haven't a clue what I was after doing. If I could have got out of there I would – I'd have climbed through the window. Anyway, we turned him over again on his back. After a couple of seconds, he lifted one leg and then the other leg. The next thing he was up and out on the floor, pain all gone. It was extraordinary.

'I've treated all sorts of people since, including politicians, but they wouldn't want their names mentioned. One time I treated a TV personality and made him better. Not long afterwards he was appearing on a programme about backs; he said he only went to properly qualified doctors and never to any place else. He was denying the evidence of his own treatment and recovery. He's been back to see me, but I've never had much time for him since.

'Now people come from all over. I had some visitors from America last week. Quite a number have come. Mostly it's back trouble. I'm not advertising there, so it must be word of mouth. I treated a nurse here from the States. She was hardly able to walk and had been off work a long time. When she went back she was able to return to work. She told everyone what had happened and quite a few came over after that.

'The farm was originally my main income, but then the bone-setting got busy. I call myself a bone-setter rather than an osteopath or chiropractor because that's the original word and that's what I do. I often thought about doing a course on it, but never did. I studied books my sister brought home from university. The more I looked, the more confused I got. I just cast them aside.'

Danny, like Tom Foley, is a long way removed from the now outdated image of the archetypal Irishman. Not a drop of the hard stuff has ever knowingly passed his lips. In fact he's a Pioneer, which means he's pledged himself never to touch it.

His stance against drink has not been taken lightly. Nor does it mean he disapproves of it: 'My uncle killed himself with it and my father drank a bit, too. He used to get very contrary with it, kind of fighting mad, and so I made up my mind not to drink. My uncle Pat never touched a drop until he was 57 – and then he never stopped. He must have been an extraordinarily healthy man before he started, because he lasted 13 years. I'm no goody two shoes, though. I wear the badge so that people can tell I don't drink and won't ask me.'

Surprisingly, in view of his success with Danoli, and unusually for a man who has spent the whole of his life in Ireland, Danny had never been a man for the horses. Until Danoli came along, that is: 'I had no interest in them. I used to think that people coming here with horses which had bad backs and legs and shoulders and dislocations were all mad. But Olivia – she was interested in horses and ponies from an early age. So we got an old pony for her to ride. She was always going on about getting a mare so she could breed from her, so one day I asked Tom Foley about getting me one.

'Nearly a year went by and nothing happened. I reminded him and Tom asked me to meet him at the Goffs sale. He couldn't find a mare but he spotted a horse that took his fancy. He told me to come and look at him, but I knew nothing about horses. "You're the fellah who's buying him," he said. "Just pretend you know something." So I went and had a look but he seemed the same to me as any other horse. Tom had a hunch about him, though. And when he got him for £7,000 I was delighted.'

If Danny thought his life had changed when he'd discovered The Gift, it was about to be shaken inside out and turned upside down as a consequence of his acquiring a horse whose fame would far outstrip his own. He and Tess set off excitedly for Tipperary to collect him. Accompanying them was Tom's brother, Ger. He knew how to handle horses. They didn't.

Tess admits: 'I ran a mile from the horse. I thought he was as mad as a hatter because they couldn't get him into the box. Then we brought him back here. It was eight o'clock in the evening. We tried to put him into the house but he was as stubborn as a mule. He wouldn't go in. It was a cattle shed and the doorway was too low. So we rang Tom and he came for him.'

Danny takes up the story: 'He kept him for a few days and took him to a fellow to break him. Then the horse was brought back here and went straight over the road with the cattle. He also spent some time with Olivia's pony. If we'd known how great he was going to be, we'd never have even let him cross the road. Jimmy and Olivia used to ride him out. They'd gallop him every morning as far as the hill, a distance of about two miles. But Olivia had to stop because the horse was too strong and keen: she couldn't hold him. Jimmy was able for him – at least for that first year. He never rode him after that.

'The fellow who buys the cattle for us asked me how much I'd paid for the horse. When I told him £7,000, he said: "You could buy plenty of oul' heifers for that." He thought it was an awful lot of money to pay for a horse. I don't suppose he thinks that now.

'Danoli was here until the end of the summer. Then Tom took him away to train and prepare him for his first bumper. The morning of the race, he told me the horse was in great form. I asked should we back him and he said: "No. It's his first race and you wouldn't know what he'd do with the crowds and everything else." But we couldn't let him go off unbacked. We had to have a little bit on. So Tess, her brother Seamus and myself all put £5 each way on the Tote and we got back around £650 between us. He was 16-1 with the bookies and we beat that by a long way.

'Tess had given Seamus a tenner to back Atours as a saver, but he handed it back and said: "Sure, you're not going to bet against your own horse."

'Before the race, Willie Austin had come up to us and said: "He'll hardly win first time out." When Danoli won, he got very disappointed and turned away from us. He'd had two horses to sell and he sold the wrong one. He realised he should have kept Danoli. But his wife was thrilled and why not? They still have Danoli's mother, Blaze Gold.'

Danny soon realised that ownership of a racehorse carried with it an obligation to the local populace to tip them the wink: 'Everybody round here was disappointed we didn't tell them Danoli would win first time out. Tom has a brother-in-law, Eamonn Quirke, who's manager of a co-op in Carlow Town. I had a message to ring him the following Monday.

'He said: "God dammit, you never told me the horse was going to win."

'I said: "How would I know, first time out? I even asked Tom if I should back him and he said no."

'Eamonn said: "Ah, don't mind that fellah. If there were two flies crawling up the wall and a lump of lead hanging from one of them, he wouldn't back the other one."'

Danny laughs loudly. It's a good-natured dig at Tom, for whom he obviously has great affection.

'The second time out Danoli was up against Sea Gale, who was the red-hot favourite. Danoli opened at 16-1 and was backed down to 10-1.

'Willie Austin came into the parade ring and said: "Do you think you'll win?"

'I said: "We hardly will, but we'll do our best." He won by four lengths, but I didn't see Willie after the race. I've met him a few times since. At first he hardly spoke at all, but he's mellowed over the years.'

Danoli's career continued and Danny experienced more good fortune with him than any first-time owner had a right to expect. Then came Aintree and there was nothing his magic hands could do to mend *that* bone. It was shattered. Dark days followed, when he never knew if the horse would race again.

The story of Danoli's return is legend. The rise and, then the falls at Fairyhouse and Leopardstown. Did Danny lose faith?

'Not for a second. You see, Tom is over-protective of Danoli. And that day at Fairyhouse, the horse was hyper. He really wanted to go. Jim Treacy was leading him round the parade ring and he had his back to the horse's shoulder with his head pulled in across him, trying to hold him. I saw on the video when Danoli was going down to the start with the mouth open and he flying. It was a real slow race and it was only his third time over fences. He became unsettled and didn't try to jump.

'At Leopardstown, it was a false start. The starter told Tommy Treacy to pull Danoli back. When he went to pull him back, the horse turned right around. As he was turning, yer man pulled the tape to start the race and Danoli was last away. Then Charlie Swan's mount cut across him and he fell. Any doubts about Danoli's jumping were well and truly laid to rest in the Hennessy. What a race and what a reception.'

Danoli had come through with flying colours: royal blue and

white, to be precise – the colours which mean so much to Danny O'Neill: 'I attended Rockwell College in Cashel, Tipperary. Blue and white were the colours of the school and the school was dedicated to Our Lady. At that time, I was taught religion; I'm very conservative and I live up to it, although I can't pretend I don't let rip with the occasional curse. The local GAA club colours are black and amber, and people from these parts couldn't understand why I didn't choose them. But the colours of Our Lady carry a special significance, I'm sure she's looking after us.'

With help from on high, then, don't bet against lightning striking twice for Danny O'Neill, the man whose healing touch has, where Danoli is concerned, turned into the Midas touch. He now has another budding star with Tom Foley – the four-year-old Dantess, as yet unraced. No prize for guessing how *he* came to be named.

'Tom thinks a lot of this one, too, but he's warned me not to expect the earth with him. He says that when you've started off with a horse as good as Danoli, it's a case of working your way back down.' We'll know shortly, on Dantess's racecourse debut, how he measures up to the star of the family. He came ready made, as it were, when, in 1993, Danny bought a mare, Kalamalka, from Aidan O'Brien's father-in-law, Joe Crowley. She was in foal to Be My Native and Dantess is the result. He was a late (May) foal and has been gelded.

Says Tess: 'You have to have them gelded or you couldn't let them near the mares. They'd be too frisky.'

She and Danny laugh. After seven children, she knows all about frisky stallions.

14
Hanging On for The Grip

THE TV people are out in force this morning. First up is Mark Saggers, senior sports correspondent for Sky News, attended by camerawoman, Zoe MacDonald. They are joined by a team from RTE's news feature programme *Nationwide*, headed by presenter Helen McInerney.

Mark and Helen want on-camera interviews; and they're keen to film you-know-who at work. They've been waiting a while because I've delayed Danoli's appearance till eleven, when a camera crew from the Irish sports programme *The Grip* is due. I can't keep bringing him out for one, putting him back in his box and bringing him back out for someone else. I'd be doing it all day long. There has to be some kind of order.

Eleven o'clock comes and goes and there's no sign of *The Grip*. I'm beginning to lose my own grip and I'm not alone: Goretti and Pat have been allowed to skip school to meet the programme's presenter, Sarah Flaherty. She's a big favourite of theirs.

Half-an-hour later, still no *Grip*. I get Danoli from his box and

Noel Hamilton mounts up. I instruct him to keep to a walk. Round and round they go in endless circuits of the wood-chip gallop, followed by the other five horses in the third lot. Another ten or 15 minutes pass and I'm concerned. I want to help the programme-makers, but not to the detriment of the horse. I've got a Gold Cup to win. Also, it's starting to rain and I won't risk Danoli catching a chill. I want him back in his box.

'They must have got lost,' I say, stating the obvious. I turn round and everyone looks glum, as if my concern is their concern. I decide to lighten the mood. 'The saying goes that you get to Newlands Cross in Dublin, take three left turns and you're here.' I say it with a grin and everybody relaxes. The truth is they'd need a compass and an orienteering map to find Aughabeg.

It's a convenient time to do the interview with Sky. Mark Saggers confides that his family runs a bookmaking business in the north-east of England. He'll know a bit about racing, then. He fires in his questions and I'm off on my favourite topic: 'Danoli has some heart and battling is what he loves . . . I'm not worried about the fences – no, not at all – Penndara definitely cut across him the last time . . . he sells a lot of coverage . . . besides the Irish, there'll be 10,000 English supporting him . . . if he's there at the death, he'll battle on up the hill . . .'

The interview over, I cast an eye up at the weather and then across at Danoli, still parading round with the rest of the string. I check my watch and give a shake of the oul' head. It's cold and drizzling and I need to get Danoli working. Helen McInerney goes into action. She phones RTE on her mobile – gets through to *The Grip* production office. She's told the crew is ten minutes away. No sooner has she finished the call than they arrive, minus Sarah Flaherty. She and co-presenter Ryle Nugent are in Paris on an athletics shoot and the interview will be conducted by the show's producer, Fiona Keane. That's fine by me, and Goretti and Pat hide their disappointment well. They say they don't mind. I know better.

I signal to Noel and the rest and the horses move down to the sand gallop. The TV people want only me and the horses and everybody else hangs back. I'm told it's a tremendous shot with 'great dramatic sweep – a man at work with his horses and riders against the backdrop of the Blackstairs Mountains.' To me it's an everyday occurrence – to them it's art, like David Lean's famous long shot in Lawrence Of Arabia.

Talking of film stars, Danny O'Neill arrives to be interviewed for *The Grip*. He waits for us to come back up and there's some banter from the work-riders – 'You put on the tie, then' and 'It'd take the TV cameras to bring you down here' – and he takes it in good part. He's not over-fussed about Danoli; he can see he's in shape. He's kept the faith in me – and the horse.

His interview with Fiona Keane includes showing off the bone-setting. He runs his fingers along the back of The Subbie, who lives next door to Danoli. This one's a Group winner over hurdles, whose chasing career was cut short by back trouble. And who better to sort it out than the owner of his nearest neighbour? 'Done you a favour there, Subbie me boy. Got Dan the man to fix up your back.'

Danny's sensitive fingers feel for the spot, the horse gives a jump and Danny announces with a knowing nod that he's found the problem. Sorting it out will wait for another time, for this little exercise is just for the cameras.

Meanwhile, Danoli, back in his box, is wondering what's going on. It's the first time a camera crew hasn't focused exclusively on him. At one stage he pops his head over the wall to see what the fuss is about: 'What are you playing at, O'Neill, stealing my thunder!'

I look in on Danoli and reflect on the previous day's comings and goings. The Eurovision Song Contest crew were here filming him for the programme. Not for the singing, you understand, but for one of the fill-in slots. When Ireland wants to show off its baubles, it calls on Danoli. They shot four-and-a-half hours' of film for two minutes of transmission. Come the show at The Point, in Dublin, he'll have a fan club half a million strong.

By two-thirty, the camera crews are gone and we can relax at last. It's time for lunch – chicken in breadcrumbs (one of my favourites), mashed potatoes and vegetables. The boys – plus Sharon and Adrienne – never take their full hour. In fact, nowhere near it. Their meals finished, they get straight back to work, brushing down the 40-odd horses housed in the two main stable blocks and the indestructible 'bomb shelters' I built when I was getting started. It's back-breaking work but it's done with a good heart. I've long been aware that this is not so much a job but a labour of love. There could be no other way of life for any of the work riders – Sharon and Adrienne included.

They earn between £80 and £120 a week – not a fortune, but they wouldn't swap places with anyone.

HALF A DOZEN horses thunder up the sand gallop. Sharon and Adrienne are aboard two of them and a mother's protective instinct comes into play. Goretti is anxious about a camera crew perched beside the track: 'They're too close. They could spook the horses.'

Thankfully, they don't. Several tons of horseflesh hurtles by and Sharon and Adrienne finish upsides each other. Their smiles say they're loving every moment. It's something they've been born to.

AS I brush down Danoli, the sheen of fitness tells me all I need to know. I read about trainers in England doing daily blood tests and the like and I don't understand it. You can tell a horse's condition just by looking at him. The coat is the tell-tale sign. It reflects his well-being. He can't look a million dollars on the outside and feel bad on the inside – it's just not possible.

I tend Danoli – some might say fuss over him – with undisguised pride. In return, he sends me flying with head-butts. That's gratitude for you.

15

We Click with the Camera Lads

GOWRAN PARK is a great little racecourse. But then I would say that, wouldn't I? It's my local track, just nine miles away in County Kilkenny on the other side of the River Barrow. Apart from providing top-class racing on the Flat and over the jumps, the atmosphere is always electric and it's one of the friendliest courses in Ireland.

Danoli loves the place. His reception when he won the Red Mills Hurdle was something special. He really comes alive when we take him there for a bit of schooling. With Tommy Tracey up, he did two important pieces of work on the course in preparation for the Gold Cup, one of them over the fences.

His jumping was fine, but he hit the last a bit of a belt and I had to tell Tommy to go back and do it again. The problem was, the horse had known it wasn't a race and lost concentration. But he jumped it fine the next time. Then he schooled well over the last three fences, again standing off as he took the last in his stride.

There are 22 big ones in the Gold Cup, so I was hoping the session would sharpen him up. It was the first time he'd seen a racecourse since winning the Hennessy and he hadn't forgotten the reception he received. I wouldn't want him so fired up at Cheltenham.

A week or so later, I took him back to Gowran for his last serious piece of work. With just three days to go before heading for England, I'd wanted only Tommy, his dad, Jim Treacy, and myself in attendance – nobody else. But I let the cat out of the bag when I schooled the horse there previously. I said I might bring him back and walk and trot him around and let him learn that he's to settle and not get agitated. They all picked up on that and when we arrived, there were already several camera lads and a television crew waiting. So was the Danoli Fan Club – a group of perfectly responsible racing people who knew these were pressure days for the horse and were there just to observe and feel part of it all. If the horse was happy to have them around, then so was I. We'd know soon enough.

I'm one of those people who finds it difficult to disguise his feelings; which means that if everybody was expecting a broad, cheery smile as I climbed down from the jeep, they were disappointed. I couldn't force a smile because I was worried that their presence might upset Danoli, when all I'd wanted was for the horse to have a quiet solo spin. I didn't want him getting excited and rearing up.

Thankfully, Danoli came down the ramp without a bother on him. He stood there nice and calm and quiet as the camera lads packed together like a rugby scrum and thrust their lenses in his direction. I was still concerned, though. If Danoli had showed any sign of temperament, I'd have loaded him straight back in the box. My first duty is to the horse and the owner and I wouldn't allow him to work himself into a lather. But as the cameras clicked and whirred, I could see there wouldn't be a problem. I became more relaxed by the minute, perhaps taking my cue from Danoli. He was as docile as could be. He knew what he was there for, but first he had to do his stuff for the camera lads and the TV cameramen – not as a racehorse but as a celebrity.

Tommy Treacy waited patiently to go to work, noting the unmistakable buzz in the air. He'd been given time off by his brilliant boss, Paddy Mullins, who'd be the first name I'd nominate as a model for any new trainer coming into the game. I'd settle for knowing everything Paddy's forgotten about racing. For him to have Tommy as first jockey proves the lad has what it takes. And his future couldn't be in better hands.

At 21, Tommy has an old head on young shoulders. And you detect a steely determination about him – a sense of destiny. I knew that whatever else happened at Cheltenham, Danoli wouldn't lack for power from the saddle. I could see, too, that Tommy was taken with the condition of the horse, and no wonder. He looked an absolute picture.

At last the photo session was over and Tommy climbed aboard Danoli. There was a sense of anticipation, a tingle of excitement. I'd told Tommy not to jump a fence with him. We'd already given him a school and his jumping in the Hennessy was practically flawless. I'd no wish to tempt fate. Instead, I told Tommy to go a good clip and to let the horse use himself.

The camera lads and the TV people moved quickly down to the course to do their filming, seeking the best possible vantage points. So did the Danoli Fan Club, full of expectancy, their binoculars at the ready. I left them all to it and hurried on alone. I knew what I was looking for and I wanted nobody's company but my own. It was a bright, sunny morning but there was a sharp wind cutting across the course that kind of made you catch your breath – but not half as much as watching Danoli. His piece of work was exhilarating. There's no other word for it. You can tell how well a horse is working just as easily from a solo spin as when he's accompanied by other horses; and Danoli was buzzing. He stretched out like a champion and I could tell full well he was enjoying himself. He and Tommy were as one, like man and machine in unison. It had been a serious piece of work and yet Danoli wasn't blowing hard enough to put out a candle. In fact he hardly broke sweat and neither did Tommy. His expression said one word: 'Wow!' It was enough to tell me Danoli was primed for Cheltenham.

I was still anxious to hear Tommy's verdict, though. I wanted to know how keen the horse was, how easily he travelled, how he responded when asked for a bit of an effort. I saw it all with my own eyes, of course, but I'm sure Ferrari ask Michael Schumacher for his opinion after a test run and act on what he says, even though, like me, they'd be pretty clued up on how things went.

Tommy's words were not for Press ears. We moved well clear and he told me just what I wanted to hear. Once we'd spoken, I talked to the paper and TV lads – but I didn't give them everything.

'He's interested even on his own now,' I told them. 'Tommy says he tried to get into one of the fences below and take it on. That's how keen he is. I'm quite happy with him. At least he was relaxing at the end there. He didn't get as worked up as he did the last day.'

At Leopardstown, when he won the Hennessy, he was as cool as could be because he'd been at Gowran a few times. We just worked him quietly, with no one else around, and he settled down calm and grand. That was why I wanted him back there that day – just to show him that every time he stepped on to a racetrack he wasn't going out to battle and take on other horses. I realised it would make a difference at Cheltenham if we could get him to settle. The problem was that we'd be there for the full three days and the Gold Cup wasn't till the Thursday. He'd hear the racing going on the other two days and start getting keyed up. You'd see him wondering, 'How come I'm not going out?' Perhaps we'd stuff a bit of cotton wool in his ears so he couldn't hear what was going on – try him that way.

We'd be bringing 60–70 gallons of water. The horses here are used to drinking pure spring water, whereas the water at Cheltenham might have chlorine in it. We couldn't take the chance. Our water is piped in from two wells – one in the yard and another out in the field and so we know it's fresh. We'd also be taking a couple of hundred pounds of Red Mills nuts. No vitamins of any kind. They're all contained in the nuts. The hay over in England is good enough, so no problem there.

TOMMY TREACY is amenable and accommodating. The love of racing runs in his family and he's proud of them all: 'My dad Jim rode seven winners as an amateur, but he didn't start till late in life and so he never turned professional. My uncle Sean rode a winner in Cheltenham, and was stable jockey to Paddy Mullins as well. My other uncle, Martin, also rode in Cheltenham; he was the only seven-pound claimer to have ridden in the Queen Mother Chase. It's been in the family since I was four and I was brought up riding ponies. I rode as an apprentice at Cordell-Lavarack's, Lord have mercy on him. When he closed up I was lucky enough to get into Mr Mullins' place.

'I rode Danoli in two hurdles races at the end of 1993, at Punchestown and Leopardstown. We won the first and came third the other time. When I lost the ride to Charlie Swan, I always hoped and prayed I'd get back on him and have a second chance. It's hard to explain how much it means to ride him in the Gold Cup. It means more to me than anything.

'Before I won the Hennessy on him, the pressure was enormous. But I didn't mind. I lay awake the night before and said to myself, "Everyone's knocking us, him and me." But I knew from riding him over hurdles and schooling him here at Gowran that he'd make a chaser and we were able to prove it at Leopardstown. You could see how relieved I was when we passed the post in front. I knew they were just silly little novicey mistakes that had caused him to fall and that it would take a bit of time. I'm delighted Tom and Danny O'Neill left me on the horse because I knew I was doing nothing wrong. They knew it, too, and they were strong enough not to bow to the pressure for a change of jockey.

'When you're up on Danoli, it's like driving a real fast sports car – the fastest on the road. You've got so much in hand and so much to play with. It's unbelievable. You'd have to know him and ride him to experience it. You can't put it into words.

'I never bother about the opposition. It doesn't matter who they are. In the Hennessy, when I was battling with horses of the class of The Grey Monk and Imperial Call, I wasn't worried about them. When your blood's up and you're mentally tuned to ride in a race, you're not thinking about other horses. Personally, myself, I'm not anyway. I knew I was being criticised and the horse was being criticised and I wanted to go out and do my best and for him to do his best, because I knew if things went right he could do it. We just gave it our all and thankfully it worked out. But I wasn't concerned about Imperial Call or any of those boys because I knew if Danoli jumped as well as we knew he could, there'd be no problems – he'd be thereabouts.

'Coming up the hill at Cheltenham, I'll have no worries about him getting the distance. He's never travelled three miles and two furlongs, but, if I had the choice of any horse in the race, it would be Danoli. I've no doubts in my mind at all that if he gets down to the last and jumps the last, it will take the winner of the Gold Cup to beat him. Anything that passes him will win. In other words, nothing will get past him.

'He's so well at the moment, he's as good as ever I've felt him. I'm very confident now and happy to be riding him. I really wouldn't trade him for any other horse. He's special, you know.'

BROUGH SCOTT, the Channel Four lad, popped over to Gowran. He fixed up some photographs for his Sunday newspaper piece. He put words there and wrote a story without speaking to me at all because I was with him the night before and we had a good old chat. It didn't look like an interview at the time, but you wouldn't know. He possibly wanted to see the horse as well and he did that and was happy. He went off then.

The Gowran Park management were wonderful. They provided whatever we wanted. It meant an awful lot in the likes of it. And they never asked for anything in return. We were to run Danoli in the Red Mills Chase there; but when it worked out that we couldn't, they never said, 'Well, sure, look it, we're after providing you with schooling facilities and the track and all and you're letting us down.' No. They said, 'You go ahead and win the Gold Cup if you're able and don't worry about us.' That was the way of it.

If Danoli won the Gold Cup, we'd say our thank you by parading him at Gowran. You take the number of people there that morning who'd just got wind that we'd be there and wanted to see him. You take what might be in it if he won the Gold Cup and was going to parade around Gowran the day after coming home. By the Lord Christ Almighty there'd be some crowd, that's what. Every young lad in the country and everyone who cared anything about racing would be in it.

The biggest danger when you're preparing a horse for the race of his life is that you might overtrain him. Danoli was in as good a shape as I wanted him. I didn't want him too ready. I wanted him a little bit under rather than a little bit over and the horse was only just coming right. I was confident he'd not gone over the top.

We had time left to do just small pieces with him. Then we'd see how he was when we got over to Cheltenham. But whatever we'd do there would be just a matter of tipping around. He'd have done everything that needed to be done before we left.

16

Who the Hell is Boris?

DATELINE Sunday 9 March 1997: Two days to the start of Cheltenham. It's so close, you can almost reach out and touch it. The milling crowds, the colour, the atmosphere, the scent of glory in the air.

Danoli's strutting his stuff this morning over at Jim Bolger's in Coolcullen. It's his final piece of work before the curtain goes up on the greatest horseracing Festival on earth. He finishes on the bridle ahead of galloping companion, Eton Gale, after giving the Strong Gale gelding his usual three lengths start.

Playing catch-up or cutting out the pace – it all comes alike. DANOLI TRAVELS SMOOTHLY. The words repeat on you until you're hypnotised by them. You wonder whether the advertising men were present at one of these gallops:

The faint echo of hoofbeats in the distance before the horses come thundering into view. Binoculars trained down the straight as Joe Fallon eases Eton Gale around the bend and motors on up the hill towards you, with Danoli in his slipstream waiting to pounce and break his heart. Noel Hamilton knows just when to produce him, just when to send him cruising past before the two of them are pulled up, their day's work done in little more than a minute.

Jim Bolger's boys look on admiringly as Danoli is walked round before being loaded up for the journey home. These are horsemen and they can read the signs: muscle tone, condition, demeanour. It's second nature to them and they like what they see. Questions are asked – 'Is that it, then, before the big race?' and 'How's the leg holding up?' – and approving noises made – 'He looks magnificent, so he does' – and you realise a fund of goodwill exists for Danoli. They stand transfixed as he's driven away, like people who have caught a fleeting glimpse of the fabled Pegasus.

Back at Aughabeg, Danoli is led down to the field for a roll in the sand. He's frisky today, going over on to his back and gyrating his body through 360 degrees, his legs in the air and his head and neck at full stretch, as if trying to watch himself at play. He's allowed to take his time and he does so, finally having to be coaxed to his feet. He celebrates his well-being with a self-choreographed Irish jig before being led back up to the 'house', where he's cleaned up, brushed down and put away.

There he'll remain until morning, when he'll be taken to the airport for the flight to England. Sweet dreams, Danoli.

BEFORE taking off for Cheltenham, there's one last duty to perform. This is a must, according to the many. An opportunity not to be missed. You haven't seen Carlow if you haven't seen Boris, they say. Boris who? Yeltsin? But he didn't get off the plane.

As gently as possible, so as not to offend, they tell you that this Boris isn't a person but a place and it's spelt not with one 'r' but two. Furthermore, you're assured, it's the best drinking town in Ireland bar none.

Armed with this knowledge, you chide yourself for having given

Yeltsin house room. Remember him getting stocious drunk on that Aeroflot jet and leaving Taoiseach Albert Reynolds and senior Irish government officials standing like lemons on the Shannon tarmac? A man who can't handle strong drink would be no use whatever in Borris.

You notice on arrival that practically every second shop is a pub, which gives the place a good head start. No wonder Denny Cordell used to drink here. Whiter Shade of Ale might have been the title of the song, had he been supping in Borris at the time.

Stepping inside Joyce's, you are greeted immediately by the proprietor's son. Brendan Joyce is a young, good-looking guy who, in addition to dispensing large glasses of the black stuff and generous tots of Jameson, runs a video store in Bagenalstown. Brendan was going steady with Breda Foley; but the word is he's pretty much steered clear of the ladies since her death.

The pub is packed and Brendan is a welcoming host. Having sold you a Danoli cap for an extortionate £23 earlier in the day, when all you'd wanted was some batteries for your voice recorder, he's entitled to be. Still, a drink or two in such convivial surroundings soon heals all ills and, before long, Brendan's appearance has taken on a radiant glow. Almost without my noticing it, he has been transformed from bandit to bráthair: a great gasúr, a supporter of worthy causes and no sluggard when it comes to standing his round. Well, you have to give him the benefit of the doubt about that, because it never actually happened.

A quick glance round tells you that this, in the main, is a young people's pub. Yet in attendance, too, are the older folk whose livers have stood the test of time and who, gratifying to see, are treated with courtesy and respect. That's the great thing about the young Irish – the way they treat their seandaoine. They have time for them and dignify them to the extent that a lifetime's experience and distilled wisdom become sublime additions to the national consciousness.

The atmosphere is boisterous but bubbly. These are mainly workaday people unwinding after a day's labour. They are good-natured and good-humoured and among their number are some racing people: greyhound trainer Paddy Ryan, famous in these parts, racehorse trainer and former jockey Sean Treacy, an uncle of Tommy, and an ex-work rider Jimmy Caulfield, who rode for Paddy Mullins.

Sean was for ten years first jockey to Paddy who's still in his seventies, churning out the winners. The highlight of the partnership was his 1977 Sun Alliance Hurdle victory at Cheltenham on Lady Elizabeth Byng's Counsel Cottage. He now trains at Borris House, a 600-acre estate steeped in the centuries-old history of the feudal McMurrough-Kavanaghs. He leases 14 boxes from Andrew Kavanagh, who – after a career as a professional jockey in England, where he rode for Lincolnshire trainer Jim Leigh – returned to Borris and set about restoring the rambling mansion to its former glory.

Danoli was once a regular at the four-furlong sand gallop at Borris House. 'Tom Foley used to bring him here about twice a week,' says Andrew, who also rode as an amateur for Paddy Mullins. 'He was planning on installing his own gallop and wanted to see how Danoli handled the surface.'

Sean Treacy has only a small string – 14 horses in all – but he achieves a respectable 18 per cent strike rate. He was confident his young, ambitious nephew would give Danoli a good, positive ride. 'Danoli's a real racehorse and Tommy's got one crack at this one. He's got to go for it.'

Jimmy Caulfield, in his late thirties, admits to being an unabashed Danoli devotee. Even Dawn Run doesn't compare in his eyes: 'Dawn Run won three Champion Hurdles (the English, Irish and French) and took the Cheltenham Gold Cup. It's a feat that will never be equalled and, as the record proves, she was a truly great racehorse. But she never touched people the way

Danoli does. Everyone in racing knows this horse is something special. I call him The Demon. He'd die rather than lose. He's a horse with a human brain. I actually believe he understands everything Tom Foley says to him. And so far he has answered every call. He's got tremendous will-power and the people recognise it. If you put him at the foot of Everest, he'd run right up it.'

And now a drum roll as you move finally to Paddy Ryan.

'You must meet Paddy,' you're urged for days on end. 'He's *such* a character.'

And there he is! Propped up against the bar at the back of the pub, holding court like a modern-day Celtic king addressing his loyal and adoring subjects.

He's somewhat different from how you imagined him after such a build-up: a tall, sturdy man in his mid-forties, studious looking with brown, wavy hair, strong lenses in his specs and, as befits a man of local lore and legend, strong drink in his hand.

You quickly learn that Paddy isn't seeking the ticket to stardom. He is polite, unexpectedly reserved and doesn't feel he has anything of great moment to say about racing in general or himself in particular.

Perhaps we have got to him early, while the genie is still in the bottle. But that would be tantamount to inferring that he can't take his drink and would be about the most insulting thing you could say about a man – especially in Borris. And in Paddy's case, it would be a long way from the truth.

He attempts to push others forward, to take a back seat and carry on doing what he does best – enjoying the craic. Modestly, he wants others to get their names up, rather than himself. And it works, for a time. Gradually though, his compelling presence at the bar, where he holds such sway, begins to overshadow all else. His powerful, resonant voice reverberates around the pub and his occasional bursts into song prompt knowing smiles.

Paddy's business is dog racing, as witness his two-and-a-half acre spread laid out in pens at Corries. He bred Fossagbeg Maid, who captured the 1996 Irish Oaks and has since been mated with Shanless Slippy, the English Derby winner of the same year. He claims he's a cousin of Michael (Lord of the Dance) Flatley, whose people hail from St Mullins, just south of Borris, and whose genius and flashing feet were responsible for the emergence of Riverdance as a cultural phenomenon.

You discover that Danoli is close to his heart: 'The horse is a legend and it's marvellous he's local. Danny O'Neill would never sell him, not for all the diamonds in the world. And it's great for Tom Foley – a small farmer with a wife and four kids, same as myself. The difference between us is that I'm a steady drinker – six to eight pints a night – and Tom's teetotal. But I didn't hold that against him. I got him his first 10 or 12 owners, all good payers. The truth is, Tom's too straight and honest to be training horses. He should be making hay while the sun shines because Danoli will only be around for another two or three years.'

On Danoli's chance in the Gold Cup, Paddy was characteristically blunt. 'Luck plays a part. He'll either win or he'll fall.'

He spoke with the voice of authority. And you figured he'd be right. One way or the other.

17
Bless this Horse

NO racehorse in history has carried more blessings than Danoli. Of that there can be little doubt. With an ally like Fr Edward Dowling, he's way out in front in the Holiness Stakes.

Fr Dowling was, for 21 years, the much-loved parish priest of Bagenalstown's imposing nineteenth century Church of St Andrew with its huge steeple, three galleries and electronic bell that chimes out on the hour every hour, reminding the community of its dominant presence in their midst.

He retired in the summer of 1996 after ministering to 6,000 parishioners spread between St Andrew's and neighbouring churches in Newtown and Ballinkillen. Now 76, Fr Dowling has become a kind of unofficial chaplain to Danoli. It started with Tom Foley asking him to bless the horse before his races. But, as Danoli's fame grew, so did Fr Dowling's, with the result that he's practically omnipresent at every photo session.

In fact, so frequent are the requests for the Kilkenny-born priest to bless Danoli that, if he charged a fee, he'd be middling rich in his retirement. Dignified in purple stole – the sign of authority and spiritual power – and armed with missal and holy water container, his picture has adorned the pages of local, national and racing newspapers, bringing him an unlikely fame.

The rite varies according to the occasion or the request, but usually takes the following form: 'May the Holy Spirit shine down on you and bless and protect you.' Fr Dowling simultaneously blesses Danoli and sprinkles him with holy water, which always succeeds in startling him. 'You'd think he'd be used to it by now,' he chuckles.

There is clearly a bond of friendship and respect between priest and trainer forged during Fr Dowling's tenure as parish priest: 'Tom's a good person and very religious. Saturday evening Mass is his favourite. The same applies to Goretti. They have a lovely family and he's such an honest-to-God type of guy. He'll never cod you at any time. Goretti loves him to dress up but he hates the old tie. He doesn't even wear it to Mass.

'He believes in the blessing for Danoli. I blessed him several times before the Hennessy and, my God, was I delighted to see him win. I've actually been threatened after blessing the horse – not by Tom or his family, of course, but out on a racetrack. I was told, "If he loses, don't show your fecking face round here." I hope he was only joking! But the Irish people have a great regard for Danoli: the name is musical and attractive and they feel they own him. Of course, there's always been a big interest in racing around these parts, mainly because of trainers like Paddy Mullins. Yet Tom comes out of nowhere with this famous horse and trumps the lot of them.'

The man must be blessed.

18
Top of the Form

FORTY-SIX boys and girls, aged four to 12, are herded into one of only two classrooms at St Finian's National School in Garryhill. It's where the reluctant Tom sat more than four decades ago.

They've been rounded up from the playground by the principal, Patricia Nolan, and assistant teacher, Carmel Brenan. They have a special assignment: to tell the world of their favourite sports star. And Fr Dowling's come to hear them, too.

Eleven-year-old Pat Foley, by virtue of being the trainer's son, gets the privilege of first call. He clearly doesn't care to lord it over his class-mates, or anybody else for that matter, confining himself to the comment that Danoli had been with the family more than five years and he couldn't imagine life without him.

The whole school – including, naturally, the teachers – believes Danoli will win the Gold Cup. There are no dissenters and faith in the horse is absolute. Have they all been got at by Pat? Should there be a Stewards' Inquiry?

Heaven forbid! Democracy rules at Garryhill. Each child is a genuine Danoli fan. They've made their own 'Good Luck' cards illustrated by drawings of him looking like anything from demon racehorse to donkey to dachshund on stilts. But no matter: the image is in the eye of the beholder. It's the thought that counts and clearly these children have their hearts in the right place.

Even the windows of the annexe, home of the school's other classroom, are plastered with the multi-coloured message: 'GOOD LUCK DANOLI', embellished with shamrock cut-outs and green, white and gold tricolours.

The class of '97 believes defending champion Imperial Call is the main danger, along with the other Irish-trained horse, Dorans Pride. Is there an English threat? 'No,' they chorus contemptibly, as if the question were an impertinence. They all know how Danoli will win – 'He'll take the lead at the second last, and there's no way he'll be passed up the Cheltenham hill.'

And so what you learn from this school full of form students is that none of them – even down to the five-year-olds – is paying lip service to the Danoli ideal. They *know* the event is the Tote Cheltenham Gold Cup, they *know* all about the distance and the opposition and they *know* precisely how Danoli should go and win his race. A question-and-answer session soon dispels any notion that theirs is a fleeting interest in the horse, fuelled by the proximity of the training quarters and the presence in the school of one of the Foley children. Their interest is real and their knowledge of the horse astounding, even down to how and where he was bought. 'Pity the poor chap who sold him,' says one wee fellow.

Some talk proudly of seeing Danoli in action at Gowran and Leopardstown. Several more – in fact half the school – want to be jockeys. Others would like to emulate Tom Foley and become trainers. They are convinced that when he reads out their cards to Danoli – as he assuredly will – the horse will understand every word. They believe he's almost human and a boy at the back is sending a treat – a bag of nuts – along with his card.

All the children will be praying: 'Please, Lord, let Danoli win.'

One revealed he'd already said it for the horse that morning. Another said he'd pray that Danoli wouldn't fall.

The subject of prayer was appropriate in the presence of Fr Dowling. He has a wonderful way with the children and it's clear they have respect and affection for him. He reveals to them that Danoli doesn't like the holy water being sprinkled on him: 'He was going to have a go at me. I'm just a blessed nuisance to him.' They enjoy the joke at his own expense.

Fr Dowling has a couple of questions of his own: 'What way does Danoli lie down?'

'He doesn't. He sleeps on his feet,' comes the answer, quick as a flash.

'Does he snore?' They all laugh.

The teachers hand round copies of the poem the children have composed and you gain the impression that the whole school has contributed lines, right down to the four and five-year-olds. It's read out in unison and with rare gusto, the 46 young voices bouncing off the walls and washing over you:

What a wonderful man is Tom Foley
For training a horse called Danoli
He made him good and fast
To race like a BLAST
And bring back Cheltenham glory

What a proud man surely is Danny O'Neill
For owning a horse so full of zeal
He put Treacy on your back
A jockey with the knack
And since that day we've never looked back

Giddy up, giddy up Danoli
Go on, go on, you can do it for Tom Foley
Glory, glory for Danoli
Best of luck in Cheltenham!

The teachers are so proud and who cares if the last line doesn't rhyme? Mrs Nolan says, 'The children think of Danoli as *their* horse. There's disappointment when he loses and, of course, they become subdued. But it doesn't last long. The excitement soon builds again.'

Come Danoli's big day, it will be at fever-pitch. And it's a racing certainty that the children will be let home early to watch it all unfold on TV. Isn't it?

Mrs Nolan and Mrs Brenan look at each other and smile. They know they have no choice. The school will be empty on the afternoon of the Tote Cheltenham Gold Cup.

19

Operation Newmarket

MONDAY 10 March 1997: We're at Dublin Airport, all set to fly to Bristol. From there we travel by road to Cheltenham. But there's a fierce problem on the plane. It's a small jet adapted for horses and there are too many on board. People that is, not horses. Dorans Pride's head lad has to stay behind and that's something nobody likes to see. Maybe he'll catch a regular flight or travel by boat.

There's another piece of drama before take-off. Fog over Cork has made Bristol doubtful. The new destination might have to be Liverpool, meaning a longer journey by road. No problem – I'm quite relaxed about it. Everything will be fine just as long as the plane doesn't start rocking about in the sky . . .

At the last minute, a message comes through: the fog is beginning to lift. Visibility should be perfect by the time we hit Cork. We'll be flying to Bristol after all.

There are seven horses on the plane, including Eton Gale. His owners are taking a chance he'll get in the Coral Cup. If he doesn't, they won't be feeling two grand. That's what it costs to transport a horse to Cheltenham.

There's a couple of seats at the back, but I prefer to stand. You're nearly more comfortable on your feet, so I position myself beside the horses. That way they won't become upset – and neither will I. Fifty minutes later, we land at Bristol. It's been a pleasant flight, if ever there was such a thing.

TUESDAY 11 March: Danoli appears to have taken the journey in his stride. We brought him out this morning and gave him a handy canter on the course. Tommy rode him and there's not a bother on him. We're not jumping him at all. We had a good look at him and thought we'd let him run on Thursday without showing him what he's got to do.

The ground will be fast. It'll dry an awful lot today under this blazing sun. I can't say it will suit us any more than the others but we won't complain. That's the way of it. He's travelled before here on fair good ground and it didn't worry us that much. The fences, though, are big – very, very big. I wouldn't have minded getting a saw this morning and cutting them down a bit. When Danoli won here in the 1994 Sun Alliance, it was over hurdles. He'll find a huge difference this time.

I think he'll take to the fences, but there are a couple of trappy ones all right. The first down the back – I think it's the third fence – could catch you out very quick. The other one is No 12 – I don't know which one that would be. But we'll take it all as it comes and I'm sure he'll jump them, no bother.

They tell me the blue-and-white bunting is out around Bagenalstown and that the whole of Carlow – and most of Ireland – is on the horse. I've been mobbed by Danoli fans here at Cheltenham. If goodwill on both sides of the Irish Sea means anything at all, he's already past the post.

Danoli is in Box 15. All the boxes are the same and a lot of the

Irish horses have been placed together. That's so the horses can have a good natter. And perhaps even the trainers. Security is so tight it's like Fort Knox. Even Danny with his gift of the gab will have a job getting in.

We'll take things as they come each day with Danoli. Walk him out and around and let him get his bearings. It'll be a little bit different tomorrow because the other lad, Eton Gale, did get in. He runs after all in the Coral Cup, although he's well out of the handicap. There are 29 going to post, so he'll need some luck in running. The horse won't mind the ground, but whether he'll jump on it is another story. He's been working well enough with Danoli, but has the problem that the odd time he does burst. If it happens in a race, you're in trouble. There's nothing you can do.

The horses are never left alone: there's always somebody with them. I'm alternating with Jim Treacy and Joe Fallon. We take turns to keep an eye on them around the clock. Danoli's no problem. He's been through it all before: he knows what he's here for. We'll wash him down today with warm water and keep him clean and cool. Tommy's riding Beakstown for Paddy Mullins today in the Arkle. We ran against him in Ireland when Danoli fell, but we beat him in the Denny Gold Medal Chase. It'll be interesting to see how he goes.*

WEDNESDAY 12 March 1997: This is Eton Gale's big day. As you know, I've been using him to sharpen up Danoli on the gallops. He can lead Danoli for about six furlongs, which proves he's got pace to burn. Danoli's still flying and he listens to what Jim Treacy, Joe Fallon and myself are saying about the Gold Cup. We're full of optimism and I'm sure it rubs off on him. We've no worries with Danoli tomorrow, apart from the ground, and I'm expecting a big run today from Eton Gale. I've advised a small

* Beakstown, a 33-1 outsider, finished seventh to the Martin Pipe-trained winner Or Royal.

each-way flutter on the horse; and if his work with Danoli is anything to go by, he could even win. But I'm aware it's a hot race with a big field of runners.

Eton Gale has drifted from 66-1 to 100-1, so it shows what faith the punters have in my judgement. If he's placed, though, anybody brave enough to back him will be in clover.

Richard Hughes, the jockey I booked at the request of the owners, has settled the horse well off the pace – in fact, too far back for my liking. When he begins his effort four furlongs out, there's a tremendous leeway to make up. But does he fly! He burns up the course and with two furlongs to go he's in with a real chance. 'Eton Gale has come from another county,' booms the course commentator.

He's made up ground hand over fist, but the effort to get to the leaders has drained him. He's unable to sustain his surge up the hill and battles on one-paced to the line. He finishes a respectable eighth – just four lengths off the winner, Big Strand. Not bad for a 100-1 shot. If only he'd been ridden closer to the pace . . . it could have been one of the biggest upsets in Cheltenham history.

The day is rounded off in brilliant style by Florida Pearl's victory in the Weatherbys Champion Bumper. It's a success for Bagenalstown, where Florida Pearl had been a huge tip flying around for months – indeed ever since his win at Leopardstown in December. Willie Mullins, his trainer, and son of Paddy, fancied him like mad. Willie trained and rode Wither Or Which to win the race 12 months ago but this time he wasn't in the saddle. He had Richard Dunwoody up and Florida Pearl led his 24 rivals a merry dance to come home five lengths clear at 6-1. I hadn't a penny on him but it sounded like the rest of Ireland did. Ah well.

It's been an eventful day. One near miss and one penalty kick without a goalie, as Declan Murphy would say. But tomorrow's the big match.

THURSDAY 13 March 1997 – It's the final day of the Festival – the day when the talking stops and the men in trilbies and their Gold Cup horses really get to work. I've never worn a trilby and I'm not going to start now. But there's a parade for the horses before the race and I do know I'll have to wear a jacket.

Danoli's had a little gentle exercise this morning. He's as sound as a church bell and we've prayed for him and prayed with him. We've talked race strategy and race tactics, too. We've told him he'll be up with the pace and that, if necessary, he'll take on the others for the lead. We might even shock everybody by leading from start to finish. Believe me, Danoli's capable of it. And once he's in front, nothing gets by.

We've shown him Page 6 of today's *Sporting Life*, headlined, 'Danoli Dream Team'. There's a photo of him with me, Danny and Tommy on it. That should gee him up. But Danoli is as right as we can get him. I can do no more. The rest is up to horse and jockey. The ground is officially good and good-to-firm in places, but it's being baked as hard as concrete by the sun. Before his injury, Danoli wouldn't have minded top of the ground. He's raced on it and won on it but those victories were mostly over hurdles. The first year we came to Cheltenham for the Sun Alliance, the ground was fine. They said it was good-to-soft, but to us it was fast. You couldn't even tip your heel down into it. So when they say in England that the ground is soft, well, to us the ground is perfect. In comparison, soft ground in Ireland is a bog.

These are big fences here. A horse has to dig deep and spring out of the ground. And when they land on the other side, it's often heavily. Horses are huge animals who carry a lot of weight and the strain on their ligaments and joints and tendons is considerable. Especially a horse like Danoli, who's suffered a serious injury. To be honest, I'd have preferred a slight bit of ease in the ground in case the leg jars up. I know Michael Hourigan is worried about the ground for Dorans Pride. He was supposed to go at Tralee the other week but they went away saying the ground wasn't right. I heard he wouldn't run unless the ground was soft and it's anything but that. But he hasn't been taken out of the race, so obviously they're going to risk him.

The parade is another concern. Danoli can be a handful at the best of times and if he gets upset or boils over, then his chance could be gone before he even gets to the start. I'll be there on one side of him and Jim Treacy will be on the other. If he begins acting up, we'll do our best to calm him. There are no guarantees in a situation like that. We'll just have to wait and see.

I don't know how the other trainers are feeling. They're probably just as nervous as I am. You can be as cool as you like in the days leading up to a big race but, come the crunch, you feel the confidence draining from you.

At the parade, the 15 runners are led single-file past the stands before they canter to the start. Danoli is behaving like a gent. He's nice and relaxed and that's half the battle with him: we'll have no excuses on that score. We reach the end of the parade, turn him and suddenly, too quickly, he's gone. No time to give the horse one last pat. No time to shout, 'Good luck!' to Tommy Treacy as the No 7 flaps slightly in the breeze and Danoli disappears into the distance.

But then how much more do we need to say and do? Sure if he's not ready now, he'll never be. One thing's for certain: if Danoli does win, they'd better not try and hold back the crowd. There'd be a riot.

A voice booms over the public address: 'They're under starter's orders and they're off!' My heart is thumping as I look for the royal blue-and-white diablo with white sleeves and that striking blue cap with a white star on top.

Winnings (even 10 per cent of £134,000) are the farthest thing from any trainer's thoughts at such a time. Prize-winning is always a secondary consideration and that's how it should be. The safety of the horse comes first – especially in such a physically demanding context. My main concern is that Danoli will be able to act on the ground. If he does, he'll jump the fences. And if he jumps the fences, he's in with a shout. That's the way of it.

Dublin Flyer is taking them along. On his tail are Mr Mulligan, Barton Bank and Coome Hill, with Danoli a close-up fifth. I'm happy enough with that, but I can sense he's not travelling. The pace is a sedate married man's gallop. The expected burn-up between Dublin Flyer and Mr Mulligan hasn't happened and I expected Danoli to be baring his teeth and pulling hard for the lead. He's jumping okay but he isn't striding out on the firm ground. The spark isn't there and I worry that the injured joint is paining him.

Tony McCoy on Mr Mulligan has taken the lead and is injecting some pace on the second circuit. Danoli is struggling to go with them; he's throwing his heart over the fences and hoping his body will follow. I know already that our Gold Cup chance will have to wait another year.

The farther they go, the more Danoli's in trouble. It's definitely the leg that's bothering him. The effort to stay in touch on the first circuit has taken its toll; the energy has drained from him and, brave as ever, he topples over at the second-last. My heart's in my boots but he and Tommy both get up, thank God. Meanwhile, Mr Mulligan runs away with the race up the hill. He wins easily by nine lengths from Barton Bank, with Dorans Pride staying on well to finish third.

Back at the stables, Danoli is in agony. I cradle his head in my arms as he lies in his box and the vet, Chris Riggs, who's come down specially from Leahurst, examines the leg. Danoli looks at me with his big, sad eyes as if to say: 'I did my best but the pain was too much to bear.'

He senses I'm pleased with his effort. How could I be anything else? Rather than pull up, he's run himself into the ground. I blame myself – the going was simply too fast. But how are you going to find out unless you run the horse? I had to let him take his chance because he'd had no difficulty before with fast ground. In fact, he loved it.

Now we'd have to rethink his future.

WE WERE to learn that it wasn't only the going that beat Danoli that day. He sustained an additional fracture to the same fetlock joint that didn't show up in the X-rays taken by the course vets after the race. These showed only that the leg was swollen and sore. Nothing else.

It was only when routine X-rays were taken by the veterinary surgeon continuing with Danoli's care in Ireland, the German-born Herr Heinrich Zieg, that the new problem emerged. It transpired that Danoli had sustained a separate chip fracture of one of the small bones of the fetlock joint. If this additional injury occurred in the heat of Gold Cup battle – and we're 99 per cent certain that it did – then it answers a lot of questions about Danoli's performance. It means that he was struggling under the burden of a double handicap. To have carried on the way he did until falling two out shows he'd not only been brave, but heroic.

I got straight on to Chris Riggs, who suggested that arthroscopic surgery to remove the chip would provide the best possible long-term solution. The operation would involve inserting a telescope into the joint and he recommended it be carried out by Mr Ian Wright, an equine orthopaedic surgeon based in Newmarket.

The date for the operation was set and Danoli travelled to England by boat on 20 May for what had been described to me as a pretty routine and straightforward piece of surgery. The operation was performed successfully and, at the same time, Chris Riggs removed the two orthopaedic screws that pinned together the joint between the cannon bone and long pastern.

Danoli flew back to Ireland from Ascot on 18 June and I was

both relieved and delighted to have him back. An added bonus – and equally as important as the success of the surgery – was the fact there was no evidence of arthritis in the joint. This had been a major concern of Chris Riggs and the team at Leahurst after the original operation. Every possible precaution had been taken to prevent it setting in and at times it had been a slow and laborious process. But it looked to have paid off.

Since the injury occurred, I've been mixing a supplement into Danoli's food called D-Flex, which it's claimed can prevent the onset of arthritis in animals. It seems to have helped and, whisper it, Danoli appears to be almost as good as new: no broken bones, no screws holding his leg together, no arthritis.

Cheltenham 1997, far from being a disappointment, may yet prove to be the turning point in Danoli's career.

20
Danoli's Kingdom

BEING a racehorse trainer isn't all excitement and glamour. Far from it. It's hard work, so it is. And sometimes you wonder why on earth you went into it in the first place. At moments like these, you get to thinking that there must be easier ways of making a living.

The feeling lasts only as long as it takes you to walk round the yard and see the faces of the horses that all those hopeful owners have placed in your care.

In addition to the 14-box stable where Danoli is housed, there's a new block almost directly opposite. It has 16 boxes – all of them occupied. Then there are the boxes constructed of breeze block with corrugated roofs. These are the ones I built myself when I was starting out and, begod, they've stood the test of time. There are ten altogether, and one of them contains Garrys Lock, owned by Mrs Dorothy Weld. After winning his two bumpers – one at the Punchestown Festival – this is rated a serious horse. We've started him chasing and in October he finished a promising third in a £20,000 race in Tipperary.

Five horses are housed in a small block next to the hay-barn and one of them is Dreamcatcher. He's our four-legged Eric Cantona, so called because he was just as wayward. Now he's a reformed character who no longer kicks and bites, though this owes more to the calming influence of my daughters Sharon and Adrienne than any words from Alex Ferguson. His improved temperament coincided, as in the case of his namesake, with a dramatic turnround in form. And it was a case of 'Ooh Ah Cantona' when the four-year-old grey stormed to victory in a bumper at Thurles, giving Adrienne her first success as a jockey. There's a big future for this Cantona, even if the French one has put himself out to pasture.

We've plenty of other budding stars and starlets, such as Hurmuzan (a winner of four out of six, including one over the Flat), our massive five-year-old Grey Skies, a nice horse in the making, and the, as yet, unraced pair Lelari and Dantess. Watch out too, for Prince Dante, who's carrying all before him. Then there's Elvis, who'll take the stage shortly under his real name God's Rock. Why the girls call him Elvis I don't know; but he does curl up his lip a bit.

I put Go Now in a Listed handicap hurdle at Listowel towards the end of September and he won by two lengths from Le Grande Bard. Barney Cordell was over for the race and he went home with the £5,780 winner's prize tucked safely in his pocket. He also backed the horse at 4-1. You could say he was a happy man.

Our older generation includes the ten-year-old French-bred Le Ginno, a top-class staying chaser owned by the Irish World Partners Syndicate. There's some good races left in him yet. He'll be tough to beat wherever we place him.

All the horses are treated equally. They get the same food, the same water, the same exercise and the same attention. But Danoli's presence stamps him head and shoulders above the rest. He's the star of our 40-strong string and, thankfully, that doesn't bother the other owners. They're proud to be part of the Danoli success story and naturally they hope some of the magic is rubbing off on their horses. I'm sure that's the case.

Danoli occupies the first box in the stable block closest to the house. This isn't because we need to keep a close eye on him particularly, but simply to make him more accessible to the army of people who come to see him. It also saves having to inconvenience the other horses in the yard. You'd see the sense of this when March comes round each year. That means the Cheltenham Festival, the summit of their dreams for every Irish owner, trainer and jockey and the period when the family and I come under the greatest strain. That's the price you pay for having a star like Danoli in your stable, especially when he's going for the race they call the most prestigious in the National Hunt calendar.

The build-up begins three weeks to a month beforehand. The phone starts ringing and it never seems to stop. Question after question, morning, noon and half the night. The demands on you increase by the day. You're torn in a dozen different directions and there's no let-up. There's hardly time to breathe. You wonder how there can be so many different newspapers and magazines, radio and TV programmes, all of them picking up on Danoli and wanting to know the smallest detail concerning him. And then there are the news programmes – dozens of them. Half the time, I'm doing interviews live over the telephone. Then the whole pack of them want to come out to Aughabeg to do this, that or the other. This has the effect of stimulating more interest and the whole thing builds up into a kind of crescendo.

Am I complaining? Why would I? In fact I look forward to it all, because to train a horse like Danoli is a privilege and a blessing, and all the attention is a reflection of the public's high regard for him. Why does it happen, year after year? I think I understand enough about it now to be able to tell you. These lads from the media know what's going on and they're cute enough to know how to tell it. As far as Danoli is concerned, they realise that this type of horse comes along once in a generation, maybe once in a lifetime. He went to Cheltenham carrying not only Tommy Treacy on his back but the hopes and dreams of the people of Ireland.

The English, too, can't resist him. Writers and TV people come over to watch him work. It's as if a whole industry grows up around him for just this one event. Throughout it all I have to keep Danoli sweet – make sure he's happy and working well and produce him fit enough to run the race of his life. Otherwise I'd get it in the ear from all those hardy souls who back him each time he runs. I find that people who bet on the horses are, in the main, good sports; if Danoli runs his race and gets beat, they don't complain. They go away, lick their wounds and live to fight another day. They know that nobody forces them to back the horse; it's their decision and they have to stand – or fall – by it.

But my thoughts are more with the ordinary men, women and children who proved their love for Danoli by sending him stacks of cards and the like when he was laid up at Leahurst. I defy anybody to pore over the hundreds of cards and see the drawings and get-well messages he received from little children and not be moved. It brings home to you that you're caught up in something far greater than the training of a racehorse; you're reaching out into the hearts and minds of people and sending them the signal that ordinary folk like ourselves farming stock – true sons of the soil – can, through hard work and faith in what they're doing, rise up above the ordinary and the mediocre and maybe work a miracle or two.

People leading ordinary, humdrum lives need heroes they can relate to. They need something to give them a lift, to take them out of themselves for a time. And whatever way it's happened with Danoli, he's become a hero to an awful lot of them. I'm aware that some – perhaps many – are life's unfortunates, and just why they should choose a horse above a footballer or boxer or the like to pin their hopes and dreams on is something I often think about. Perhaps it's the courage and nobility of a horse like Danoli; he can't speak or communicate in the ordinary sense but he gets through to people in other ways.

I sometimes wonder, if horses could talk, whether the rest might be telling me they're fed up to the back teeth with the seemingly never-ending stream of Danoli fans who somehow find their way to Aughabeg. Nobody likes to feel left out and that applies to horses as much as humans. They're just big babies at heart. When they're feeling sorry for themselves, you'd be surprised what a couple of carrots, a pat on the head and a few affectionate words will do. They may not be versed in the English – or Irish – language, but I'm convinced they understand what you're saying. You couldn't get a better example of that than Danoli.

He's an imposing horse physically, 16.2 hands high and well-furnished with it. What stands out to me about him is the intelligent, good-looking head that attracted me to him in the first place. All top-class horses appear to have this characteristic, which explains why I've yet to see an ugly champion.

Danoli knows he's a star. It shows in everything he does, at home and at the racecourse. I suppose the best way to describe him in human terms is that he's high on confidence and self-esteem. In fact I'd call it a superiority complex. If I had to compare him with any sports superman of recent years, I'd say he was an equine Muhammad Ali. He has the same majesty, the same aura of greatness, the same outstanding ability.

There's another vital ingredient: Pride. We saw it in Ali's epic battles with Joe Frazier and George Foreman. And we saw it in Danoli's famous victories at Cheltenham and Aintree.

I'm sure Ali had to reach deep down into his soul and summon reserves of courage and spirit that, until the moment of truth, he never knew he possessed. He said that in one battle with Frazier

– when he was trapped on the ropes and Smokin' Joe was firing in power-packed punches to his head and body – he felt close to death. Imagine that. But he fought back and won. To me, that's the true mark of a great champion. In the end, Ali paid a great price. Perhaps Danoli will. I pray that he won't.

Take a close look at Danoli next time he runs. You'll see his long head thrust forward and his teeth bared as he fights to secure the victory he feels is rightfully his. I believe this unquenchable spirit touches people. Whether they've backed him or something else in the race is immaterial; they sense that this is a horse who'd rather have his heart cut out than lose.

You can guess from everything I've said that I'm immensely proud of Danoli. The horse is too good for me to say how good he is. I've never had one like him and I never will again. He's become an important part of our lives and it's a fairy-story come true for us. From being a horse nobody wanted – and a horse, his owner, Danny O'Neill, had not even contemplated buying – he has become one of racing's best-loved characters. And that love comes to him from children as well as adults. Take Paul Minchin, for example. He's only eight and he suffers from cystic fibrosis, although you'd never know it. He's as brave as Danoli, and perhaps it's what drew the two of them together.

Paul was on a pilgrimage to Lourdes when Danoli was laid up with his injury. Nobody knew whether the horse would race again, but Paul was determined that he would. So when he knelt at Our Lady's grotto, he forgot all about his own illness and prayed instead for Danoli. I know from the countless cards and messages Danoli received that there were hundreds of people praying for him and I'll be eternally grateful to them all. I'm certain in my own mind, however, that Paul's devotions from Lourdes were a big factor in Danoli's recovery.

His parents, Peter and Margaret, live close by. He has four brothers and a sister and there's not a thing wrong with any of them, so far as I know. They're able to play all the games and sports that normal children play. But Paul can't do that and I know his real love is watching Danoli. Margaret told me that the very first prayers he uttered on visiting the grotto were for Danoli to get well. She said he watched the other pilgrims kneel in prayer. Then he got down himself and asked God to make the horse better. He also lit candles for him. Well, all I can say is that Paul's prayers were answered. I'm very, very thankful and so, I know, is Danny O'Neill. It makes me feel humble when I realise that the simple faith of a child can prove so powerful.

Paul often comes over to the stables to see the horse and, of course, we make an old fuss of him. He missed Danoli so much when he wasn't here; it would break your heart to see him standing there, staring at the empty box. But when the horse returned with his leg all bandaged up, it was as if he knew his prayers had been answered.

Our local paper, the *Carlow People*, did a big piece on Paul and it was picked up by a national newspaper, the *Star*. We had a call shortly before we were due to leave for Cheltenham, asking if they could send down a reporter and camera lad. We could have done without this so close, but I agreed because the more publicity Paul receives the more it might count if appeals have to be made to help him, or others like him.

Talking of appeals, they're well on target to raising £1 million by the end of the year for jockey Shane Broderick, paralysed in a fall. We've been pleased to play our part. The crowds flocked to Down Royal in Northern Ireland when they heard Danoli was being paraded during racing. We also took him to Sue Bramall's open day at her training quarters in Inch, Co Wexford. I've no idea how much was raised and it doesn't really matter. Every little helps. The examples of Paul and Shane act as an inspiration. They remind us that nothing in life should be taken for granted.

For example, I know how easy it is to forget that I'd be much the poorer without the love and support of my family. Goretti is somehow able to combine her role as wife and mother with running our racing operation here at Aughabeg with an efficiency that I can only stand back and admire. Without her steady hand on the tiller, I'm sure we'd have gone under more than once. In addition to handling things like the race entries and the invoicing and the manning of the telephones, she cooks breakfast, lunch – including lunch for all the stable lads – and dinner, does the washing and ironing and somehow finds time in between to collect the children from school. I'm trying to find something else for her to do in her spare moments, in case she becomes bored.

Sharon and Adrienne are chips off the old block, at least as far as their love of horses is concerned. Thankfully, they've inherited their mother's looks and personality. That's balanced things out a bit.

The girls ride out for us, usually four or five lots a day, and both are excellent horsewomen. Adrienne is already showing great promise as a jockey. Her first ride in public at Fairyhouse, when she brought Dreamcatcher home in fourth place in a hot bumper, brought rave reviews. One of them said she 'displayed all the attributes of a veteran'. She has since won three races – all of them bumpers. In addition to her victory at Thurles on Dreamcatcher, she has twice won on Hurmuzan, at Gowran and Tipperary. There's not too many would fancy riding out Danoli, either. It's a big responsibility. But Adrienne wasn't intimidated. She'd say, 'My hands are sore – he's pulling too hard.' But at least she was brave enough to have a go. One day, perhaps, she'll be riding one of my Champion Hurdle or Gold Cup horses at Cheltenham. Times are changing fast in racing; there are some capable women jockeys around and trainers everywhere are taking note.

Sharon, too, is a fine rider. She holds an amateur licence but has no plans to go public. Her leanings are more towards tending the horses. She has a great way with them and maybe she'll eventually take after her dad and become a trainer. Whatever the way of it, it looks as if the Foley name will be to the fore for quite a few years to come.

We're at the start of a new era now with Danoli. I'm convinced his problems are all behind him and the future is full of promise. We've great faith in him still and, as we've proved already, faith can move mountains. While we're on that subject, the breathtaking Blackstairs Mountains – at which I'm gazing so fondly as I speak – will again provide the backdrop as the next dramatic scenes unfold in Danoli's career.

One of the foothills – we call it 'The Hill' – is where we run Danoli up and down. 'Put Danoli at the foot of Mount Everest and he'd run up it,' Jimmy Caulfield said. Well, let me tell you: this is Everest, without the glaciers. Whenever we pit Danoli against other horses, we give them a dozen lengths start and he catches them every time. Six furlongs, straight up into the sky. Then he comes down and does it again . . . and again. There's no stopping him. He'd run up it till he drops.

He's the King of the Hill, the Master of the Mountains. From his vantage point at the top, all Carlow is his kingdom.

There's a whole world still to conquer.

The Last Word

YES, I do pray. Every day. And I do ask for things. You don't get everything you want, but you might not be granted anything if you didn't pray. So I pray.

I think sometimes you're denied what you want because it might not be best for you at the time. It doesn't mean that your prayers haven't been heard. But I just hope He agrees Danoli should win the Gold Cup in 1998. I prayed that he'd win the Hennessy and I said at the time that I wouldn't want to be greedy and ask for both. So perhaps I was taken at my word. It would be nice to win the Gold Cup all right, but if He looks after the horse and the horse is good and safe, and runs his race, he doesn't have to win to satisfy me. It's not crucial.

Some people think that seeking divine guidance overall is the way and we should leave it at that. But it's not my way. I just come right out and ask for what I want: I go straight to the front door and knock. Maybe some people like going in through the back door and asking for things that way, but generally I like going through the front door.

I believe prayer does work. You can't expect favours every day of the week because there are an awful lot of people in the world and things have to be shared around. You have to be picked and chosen according to how things are at the time. Having said that, I can't believe any horse in the Gold Cup will have as many people praying for him as Danoli: the schoolkids, the little man with cystic fibrosis, the priest, me and my family, the people of Bagenalstown and Carlow – he won't lack help in that direction, I'm sure. Everywhere he goes, people say they'll offer up a prayer for him on Gold Cup day. So that will give him one route.

But the other horses will have people praying for them, too, and maybe there'll be big bets placed on some of them. Who knows how it will all work out? As I said, I'll be happy as long as he comes home safe. That's even more important than winning.

If God grants me that, I'll be content enough.

Glossary

Boots – plastic coverings to protect a horse's shins and tendons.

Luck money – the refunding by the seller to the buyer of a portion of the purchase price. This is deemed to bring both parties good luck.

Craic – crack (chat, fun).

Bumper – a National Hunt Flat race.

Pulled in – brought before the stewards.

The 'office' – the go-ahead.

Layers – bookmakers.

Haymaker – a knockout punch.

Spoofer – hoaxter.

Bráthair – brother.

Gasúr – boy.

Seandaoine – old people.

Shebeen – illicit drinking den.

Early toe – speed in the early part of a race.

Declare a horse – register it as a definite runner.

Cat – awful.

Do us for toe – outsprint us.

Out of the handicap – rated below the official handicap mark for a particular race and having to make up the weight.

A horse 'bursts' – breaks a blood vessel.

Danoli on the Record

1992				
31 October	**Philip McCartan Memorial Flat Race (2m)**			
Naas	1st	Mr P English	16-1	£3,105
1993				
30 January	**Irish National Bookmakers Flat Race (2m 3f)**			
Naas	1st	Mr P English	10-1	£3,795
21 February	**Irish National Bookmakers Flat Race Final (2m)**			
Punchestown	1st	Mr P English	5–2F	£4,830
16 November	**Curragha Maiden Hurdle (2m 4f)**			
Fairyhouse	1st	C Swan	4-6F	£3,105
5 December	**Ballycaghan Hurdle (2m)**			
Punchestown	1st	T Treacy	8-11F	£3,105
27 December	**The 1st Choice Novice Hurdle (2m 2f)**			
Leopardstown	3rd	T Treacy	4-5F	£700

1994

23 January **AIG (Europe) Champion Hurdle (Grade 1) (2m)**

Leopardstown 2nd C Swan 12–1 £12,000

13 February **Deloitte and Touche Hurdle (2m 2f)**

Leopardstown 1st C Swan 4–5F £13,000

16 March **Sun Alliance Novice Hurdle (Grade 1) (2m 5f)**

Cheltenham 1st C Swan 7–4F £39,504

9 April **Martell Aintree Hurdle (Grade 1) (2m 4f)**

Aintree 1st C Swan 9–2 £30,585

6 November **Morgiana Hurdle (Grade 2) (2m 2f)**

Punchestown 1st C Swan 1–5F £9,675

4 December **Hattons Grace Hurdle (Grade 1) (2m 4f)**

Fairyhouse 1st C Swan 4–6F £25,800

28 December **Bord na Gaeilge Christmas Hurdle (2m 6f)**

Leopardstown 2nd C Swan 1–2F £1,550

1995

14 March **Smurfit Champion Hurdle (Grade 1) (2m 110y)**

Cheltenham 3rd C Swan 4–1JF £18,855

8 April **Martell Aintree Hurdle (Grade 1) (2m 4f)**

Aintree 1st C Swan 2–1JF £30,610

1996

21 January **AIG (Europe) Champion Hurdle (Grade 1) (2m)**

Leopardstown 3rd T Treacy 10–1 £4,500

17 February	**Red Mills Trial Hurdle (Grade 3) (2m)**			
Gowran Park	1st	T Treacy	2–5F	£6,850
12 March	**Smurfit Champion Hurdle (Grade 1) (2m 110y)**			
Cheltenham	4th	T Treacy	5-1	£9,935
30 March	**Martell Aintree Hurdle (Grade 1) (2m 4f)**			
Aintree	3rd	T Treacy	5-2F	£6,642
1 November	**Captain Christy Beginners Chase (2m 4f)**			
Clonmel	1st	Mr P Fenton	4-5F	£2,568
9 November	**Quinns of Naas Novices Chase (2m 40y)**			
Naas	1st	T Treacy	2-7F	£4,795
1 December	**Chiquita Drinmore Novices Chase (Grade 1) (2m 4f)**			
Fairyhouse	Fell	T Treacy	100-30	
26 December	**Denny Gold Medal Chase (Grade l) (2m 1f)**			
Leopardstown	1st	T Treacy	5-2F	£22,750
1997				
19 January	**Baileys Arkle Challenge Cup Chase (Grade 2) (2m 1f)**			
Leopardstown	Fell	T Treacy	9-10F	
2 February	**Hennessy Cognac Gold Cup (Grade 1) (3m)**			
Leopardstown	1st	T Treacy	6–1	£62,500
13 March	**Tote Cheltenham Gold Cup (Grade 1) (3m 2f)**			
Cheltenham	Fell	T Treacy	7-1	
			Total	**£320,759**

Meet the Family

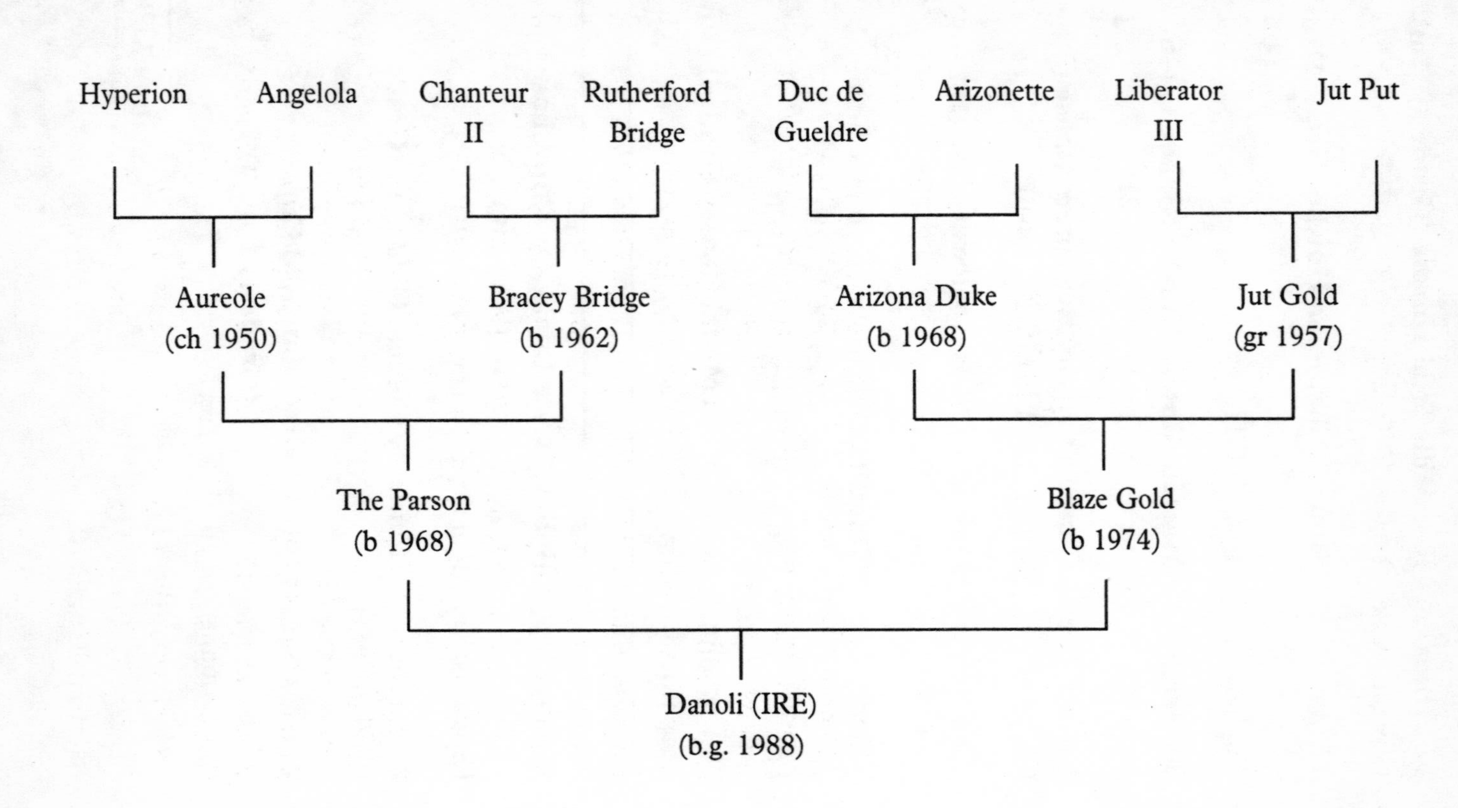

Index

Absalom's Lady, 74
Adams, Bryan, 64
Adams, Paul, 86
Aiguiere, 60
Alderbrook, 74, 90, 93
Ali, Muhammad, 170, 171
Allen, Bert, 29
Ambitious Fellow, 40
Atours, 30, 31, 67, 69, 74, 130
Austin, Willie, 26, 27, 130, 131

Baba Karam, 58
Bailey, Kim, 74
Baker, Chet, 57
Banks, Bessie, 57
Barton Bank, 163
Beakstown, 109, 112, 159
Beaumont, Peter, 112
Belmont King, 112,
Be My Native, 132
Bennett, Paddy, 19,
Berry, Jack, 59
Big Strand, 160
Blackwell, Chris, 58
Blaze Gold, 26, 130
Bold Boss, 74
Bolger, Jim, 28, 145, 146
Bono of U2, 60
Boro Eight, 4, 5
Bramall, Sue, 172
Brenan, Carmel, 153, 156
Broderick, Shane, 172
Busey, Gary, 57
Byng, Lady Elizabeth, 148

Cale, J J, 57
Camflower, 22
Cantona, Eric, 167

Caulfield, Jimmy, 148, 174
Cecil, Henry, 111
Charlton, Jack, 16
Clower, Michael, 36, 70, 92
Cocker, Joe, 57
Collier Bay, 88, 89, 93
Comerford Brothers, 95
Consharon, 96, 97, 99, 100, 104
Coolidge, Rita, 57
Coome Hill, 163
Coq Hardi Affair, 43
Cordell-Lavarack, Barney, 59, 60, 167
Cordell-Lavarack, Denny, 55–60, 62, 142, 147
Corrouge, 49, 54, 101
Counsel Cottage, 148
Crossfarnogue, 106, 109
Crowley, Joe, 132

Dantess, 132, 167
Dawn Run, 4, 50, 92, 101, 148
December Run, 18, 19, 21
Deep Endeavour, 19
Deep Run, 18, 19
Destriero, 74
Dillon, Mike, 90
Diplomatic, 34, 66
Dobbin, Tony, 114
Doherty, John, 99, 103
Dollard, John, 86
Donohue, Tom, 18, 21–3
Doran, Tom, 69
Dorans Pride, 3, 4, 49, 68–70, 72, 101, 107, 157, 161, 163
Dorking, 22
Dowling, Fr. Edward, 151–2, 155
Doyle, Jack, 48
Dreamcatcher, 167, 173
Dreaper, Jim, 112
Dublin Flyer, 163
Dunwoody, Richard, 70, 107, 111, 113, 160

Edwards, Professor Barrie, 8
Elizabeth Queen, The Queen Mother, 50, 51
Elsworth, David, 68
English, Padraig, 30, 31, 34, 35
Eton Gale, 145, 157, 159, 160

Faithfull, Marianne, 60
Fallon, Joe, 145, 159
Fallon, Kieren, 111
Fambo Lad, 36
Fame, Georgie, 57
Fawcus, Charles, 89
Fenton, Philip, 97–9
Ferguson, Alex, 167
Flaherty, Sarah, 133, 134
Flakey Dove, 52
Flatley, Michael, 150

Florida Pearl, 160
Foley, Adrienne, 17, 39, 103, 136, 167, 173
Foley, Anne, 53
Foley, Breda, 63, 64, 147
Foley, Breda Snr, 64
Foley, Ger, 11, 13, 63, 64, 129
Foley, Ger Jnr, 64
Foley, Ger (family friend), 77
Foley, Goretti, 11, 16, 17, 21, 39, 51, 52, 53, 82, 108, 136, 152, 173
Foley, Goretti Jnr, 17, 30, 31, 133, 134
Foley, Jim, 11, 13, 63
Foley, John, 11, 13, 51, 82, 83
Foley, Mary Snr, 11
Foley, Mary, 11, 13
Foley, Pat, 11, 13, 18, 21, 53
Foley, Pat (son), 17, 133, 134, 152, 153
Foley, Robert, 82
Foley, Sharon, 17, 39, 136, 167, 173
Foley, Tom Snr, 11
Foreman, George, 170
Fortune And Fame, 41, 52–4, 74, 87
Fossabeg Maid, 150
Frazier, Joe, 170

Garrys Lock, 166
Gill, Padraic (Padge), 18–21
Gimme Five, 48
God's Rock, 166
Go Now, 61, 167
Gorinski, 59
Granville Again, 29, 74
Grease Band, 57
Grey Skies, 167

Hall, Robert, 60
Hallbrook, Martin, 28
Hamilton, Noel (Hammie), 39, 83–5, 134, 146
Harrington, Jessica, 37
Haughey, Charlie, 34
Heffernan, Jimmy, 127
Horgan, Trevor, 37
Hotel Minella, 33, 34, 87–91, 102
Hourigan, Ger, 94
Hourigan, Lucy, 94
Hourigan, Michael, 3, 4, 68, 71, 72, 161
Hughes, Richard, 160
Hurmuzan, 167, 173
Hurt, John, 60

Idiot's Venture, 43
Imperial Call, 112, 114, 143, 154
I'm Supposin, 100

Jazilah, 74
Jeffell, 108

Jodami, 112, 114
Joyce, Brendan, 147
Jupiter Jimmy, 92

Kalamalka, 132
Kavanagh, Andrew, 148
Kavanagh, Richie, 53
Keane, Fiona, 134, 135
Kidd, Roly, 2
Kinane, Mick, 111
Knottenbelt, Dr Derek, 2

Land Afar, 74, 108, 109
Large Action, 4, 73, 74
Lean, David, 135
Le Ginno, 167
Le Grande Bard, 167
Leigh, Jim, 148
Lelari, 167
Llewellyn, Carl, 49

MacDonald, Zoe, 133
Magee, Sean, 101
Magic Feeling, 70
Maguire, Adrian, 41, 110, 111
Marley, Bob and The Wailers, 58
Merry Gale, 112, 113
McCartan, Philip A, 31
McCoy, Tony, 107
McCullagh, Niall, 58
McElroy, Damien, 68, 97
McGuinness, Paul, 60
McInerney, Helen, 133, 134
McManus, J P, 48
Miinnehoma, 52
Minchin, Margaret, 171, 172
Minchin, Paul, 171, 172
Minchin, Peter, 171
Minella Lad, 37, 38
Mister Donovan, 49
Modest, 58
Mole Board, 53, 74
Montelado, 74
Moody Blues, 57, 60
Moon Man, 86, 87, 95
Moore, Arthur, 30, 108
Mr Mulligan, 163
Mr Frisk, 75
Mucklemeg, 51
Mud Crutch, 57
Mulhern, John, 34
Mulligan, 110, 111
Mullins, Paddy, 4, 140, 142, 148, 152, 159
Mullins, Tony, 22
Mullins, Willie, 160
Murphy, Brendan, 58
Murphy, Declan, 28, 160
Murphy, Ferdy, 28
Murphy, Humphrey, 30
Muse, 53
Mweenish, 22
Mysilv, 4, 74, 93

Nicholls, Paul, 106

Nicholson, David, 110
Niniski, 60
Nolan, Pat, 51
Nolan, Patricia, 153, 156
Nugent, Ryle, 134

O'Brien, Aidan, 33, 35, 87, 89, 91, 93, 96, 97, 100, 102, 110, 132
O'Dwyer, Conor, 86
O'Grady, Edward, 33, 36, 51, 98, 104
O'Hehir, Tony, 97
Old, Jim, 89
O'Neill, Anne, 121
O'Neill, Bernie, 124
O'Neill, Clare, 122
O'Neill, Dan Snr, 121
O'Neill, Dan, 122,
O'Neill, Danny, 2 ,10, 12, 16, 24, 26-29, 31, 34, 40, 47, 50, 53, 61, 65, 66, 70, 72–4, 77, 94, 102, 103, 109, 112, 115, 117, 118, 120, 121, 126, 128, 132, 135, 143, 150, 155, 159, 171, 172
O'Neill, Danny Jnr, 124
O'Neill, Gretta, 122
O'Neill, Jimmy, 122, 129
O'Neill, Margaret, 121
O'Neill, Mary, 121
O'Neill, Mary (nee Brennan), 121, 122
O'Neill, Mary, 122,
O'Neill, Olivia, 53, 122, 124, 128, 129
O'Neill, Pat, 125, 128
O'Neill, Tess, 55, 119, 120, 122-5, 130
O'Neill, Treasa, 122
Or Royal, 159
Osborne, Jamie, 89, 108
O'Sullivan, Irene, 64
O'Sullivan, Rose, 64
Oxford Lunch, 95, 96, 99

Padre Mio, 41
Penndara, 110, 111, 112, 134
Petty, Tom and The Heartbreakers, 57
Pick, Ernie, 74
Pimberley Place, 69, 70
Pipe, Martin, 29, 159
Pitman, Jenny, 8
Prendergast, Kevin, 100
Pridwell, 93
Procul Harum, 57

Rebinski, 59
Reynolds, Albert, 147
Rice, Yvonne, 2
Richard, Cliff, 57
Richards, Gordon, 112
Riggs, Dr Chris, 8, 9, 77–9, 82–85, 163, 164
Ross, Ian 'Flipper', 58

Royal Athlete, 8
Rua Batric, 19, 20, 52
Russell, Leon, 57
Ryan, Paddy, 148, 149

Saggers, Mark, 133, 134
Schumacher, Michael, 141
Scott, Brough, 144
Scudamore, Peter, 70
Sea Gale, 33, 131
See More Business, 107
Shanless Slippy, 150
Shawiya, 40, 41
Sherwood, Oliver, 4
Shortt, John, 38
Simon, Carly, 123
Smurfit, Michael W J, 41
Snow, Phoebe, 57
Some Skunk, 58
Sound Man, 36, 37, 43, 48
Starr, Freddie, 52
Strong Gale, 145
Strong Promise, 93
Sutherland, Fergie, 112
Swan, Charlie, 4, 5, 35, 36, 37, 40–3, 47, 50, 51, 53, 66, 67, 71, 74, 87, 89, 91, 93, 96, 97, 99–104, 110, 111, 131, 142
Taaffe, Pat, 39
Taaffe, Tom, 39
Theatreworld, 100
The Cranberries, 59
The Grey Monk, 112–114, 143
The Move, 57
The Parson, 26
The Subbie, 135
Tiananmen Square, 91–92
Time For A Run, 51
Toots and The Maytals, 58
Treacy, Jim, 37, 58, 60, 131, 139, 142, 159, 162
Treacy, Martin, 142
Treacy, Sean, 142, 148
Treacy, Tommy, 37, 38, 39, 40, 58, 87, 88, 90, 91, 96, 104–9, 169

Ulay, 18, 19
Urubande, 93

Walsh, Ted, 60
Webber, John, 22
Webber, Paul, 108
Weld, Dermot, 41
Weld, Dorothy, 166
Winter Belle, 38
Wither Or Which, 160
What A Question, 37, 43
Wright, Ian, 164

Yeltsin, Boris, 146
Young Bavard, 20

Zieg, Heinrich, 164